KING OF COOL
WILL SMITH
BRIAN J. ROBB

Plexus, London

Published by Plexus Publishing Limited
55a Clapham Common Southside
London SW4 9BX
020 7622 2440 (telephone)
020 7622 2441 (fax)
First printing 2000

British Library Cataloguing in Publication Data

Robb, Brian J
   Will Smith : King of Cool
   1. Smith, Will 2. Entertainers - United States - Biography
   3. Rap musicians - United States - Biography 4. Motion
   picture actors and actresses - United States - Biography
   I. Title
   791'.092

ISBN 0 85965 281 5

Cover photo by Retna/T.Eric Monro
Printed in Great Britain by Hillman Printers
Cover & book design by Phil Gambrill

Thanks to the following photographers, photographic
agencies and film companies for supplying photographs:
Retna/T.Eric Monroe for the cover photograph, All Action, All
Action/Foto Blitz, All Action /Jean Cummings, British Film
Institute/National Film Archive, Corbis/Todd Gray, Corbis/Neal
Preston, Corbis/David Anderson, Everett/Corbis, Retna/Bernhardt
Kuhmstedt, Retna/Theodore Wood, Sportsphoto/Graham Whitby,
Imagenet, Columbia Tristar International Television, Twentieth
Century Fox, Touchstone Pictures and Jerry Bruckheimer Inc, Warner
Bros, Metro Goldwyn Mayer, Inc, Buena Vista Pictures, Dreamworks
Distribution, Icon Entertainment International, and Premier
Media Partners.

10 9 8 7 6 5 4 3 2 1

INTRODUCTION

Will Smith is a driven man, determined to carry out his master plan to be 'the best' at whatever he turns his talents to, whether in the fields of rap music, television or blockbuster movies. As the star of three summer box office hits in four years (*Independence Day, Men in Black* and *Wild, Wild West*) Will Smith has been dubbed 'the King of the Fourth of July Blockbuster'.

But acting the cool fool in mega-grossing movies is far from the only string to his bow. Will's career began in rap on the streets of Philadelphia in the early eighties, just as rap was crossing over from being an urban phenomenon into mainstream pop culture. In the right place at the right time, Will Smith coasted the crest of the wave with a boy-next-door image that would make him a millionaire by the age of eighteen.

For most young stars, that would have been enough – but for Will Smith, it was only the beginning. With Jeff Townes, known as DJ Jazzy Jeff, he became the friendly face of rap, fronting a series of teen-targeted, award-winning hit singles such as 'Girls Ain't Nothing But Trouble' and 'Parents Just Don't Understand'.

Will's unthreatening nice guy image allowed him to reach levels of popularity denied to the hardcore or 'gangsta' rappers who were too often associated with crime, drugs, violence and sexism to break through to mainstream popularity. 'I could never understand these guys that make rap records that are nothing but swearing and killing and misogynistic ranting,' the family-oriented rapper later explained. 'I can't imagine that the mothers of these gangsta rappers are at work and their son's record comes on the radio, and she's telling her co-workers, "Oh, y'all listen – this is my baby's new record. It's called 'Dirty Nasty Muthafucka'. That's my baby. Oh listen, now he's singing about some bitch he met." I just never want my family to be embarrassed like that.'

Along with success and fame came money – an irresistible temptation to any spendthrift eighteen-year-old. Will embarked on a year of extravagant spending before crashing down to earth, when a huge tax bill wiped out his fortune.

Offered a shot at fronting his own situation comedy on nation-wide television, Will jumped at the chance – even though the nearest he had come to acting lessons was with Jeff Townes in their music videos. It was veteran record producer Quincy Jones who rode unexpectedly to the rescue. Will still remembers the phone call from Hollywood that turned everything around. 'Come on out here, boy, and let's start the rest of your life,' the musical impresario instructed him. Sensing a second chance at fame and fortune, he declared himself better prepared this time around.

'I love the fact that I'm black in Hollywood.'

Taking the lead role in *The Fresh Prince of Bel-Air* sitcom at age 21 (though his character was considerably younger), Will began to develop a media masterplan. By the end of the series' six-year run, Will Smith had mutated into a master media manipulator – plotting to steal the box office crown from white mainstream superstars like Tom Hanks, Tom Cruise and Mel Gibson.

After a couple of false starts, Will made a huge critical impact in *Six Degrees of Separation* (1993) by playing a gay conman who talks his way into the lives of an upper-class New York socialite family. The film showed the kid from the TV sitcom had what it took to hold his own against a veteran acting talent like Donald Sutherland, but the film failed to smash any box office records.

In order to achieve his aim to be 'the best of the best', Will Smith had to take a more measured route to the top, using the action vehicle *Bad Boys* (1995) as a stepping stone to blockbuster stardom. 'The goal was to become the biggest actor in Hollywood,' Will candidly admitted. 'During the years of *The Fresh Prince* I studied entertainment thoroughly. Every step was a calculated step. For example, I looked at trends. I looked at the top ten movies of all time, and seven of them had creatures in them: *ET, Jurassic Park, Close Encounters of the Third Kind, Jaws.* It was like, okay, let's make movies that have creatures in them.'

The plan which Will drew up led to the blockbuster triple bill of *Independence Day* (1996), *Men in Black* (1997) and *Wild, Wild West* (1999). These cartoon-style performances were a million miles from his role in *Six Degrees of Separation*, but they helped to turn Will Smith into the biggest box office star of the late twentieth century.

Along the way, Will faced the problems of being a black actor in a predominantly white film industry. 'I love the fact that I'm black in Hollywood,' he has said, typically refusing to let race stand in the way of his ambitions. 'When you're the underdog you can say anything, you can do anything, because you're not expected to win. You have absolutely nothing to lose. Leonardo DiCaprio has a more difficult time staying in his position than I have staying in mine because, well, I'm not expected to be here in the first place.'

Will Smith's appeal works across the board, in music, television and movies. He has triumphed in fields in which his movie-star rivals have never even dabbled – it's unlikely Tom Cruise will ever make an award-winning gold album for example. Will's ability to laugh at himself and the world around him, and to share that laughter with audiences across the planet, has made him a star. His driving force is the work ethic and discipline he inherited from his ex-Air Force father, and the common-sense approach to life his mother instilled in him. While Will's relationship with his parents is a fraught and complicated one, it is behind his need to succeed in every field to which he applies himself.

Personally, Will Smith has paid the price for his success. After a few short-lived relationships he married Sheree Zampino and had a son, named Trey, only for the union to collapse under the pressure of his workload. Committed to his son, Will made his birth and his parents' divorce the central theme of his hit single 'Just the Two of Us'. Now married for a second time, to actress Jada Pinkett, and with a second young son, Will's private life appears to have become more secure since the more turbulent mid-nineties.

Popularity can only get you so far in Hollywood – sheer talent must do the rest. The challenge ahead for Will Smith is to show he can do more than simply 'wow' world-wide movie audiences by battling comic-alien forces and looking good in Rayban shades. *Six Degrees of Separation* and parts of the surveillance thriller *Enemy of the State* (1998) hint at a deeper talent that is, as yet, unexplored. As his *Fresh Prince* co-star James Avery says: 'I think there's a lot more going on there than anybody knows. I think there is a lot more going on there than he is really aware of.' The biggest prize still awaits Will Smith – a Best Actor Oscar, early in the new century perhaps?

01

AIN'T NO PLACE LIKE HOME

Born Willard C. Smith II on 25 September 1968 in West Philadelphia, Pennsylvania, Will Smith was the second child of Caroline and Willard C. Smith senior, joining older sister Pamela and later followed by twin siblings, Ellen and Harry.

His perfectly ordinary background was as far removed from a movie superstar's background as possible. His father owned a refrigeration company called Arcac which supplied supermarkets with chill cabinets and freezer equipment, while his mother worked as a school administrator for the local Board of Education. The family lived in a solid middle-class area of Philadelphia called Winfield, where people were comfortable, being neither particularly wealthy nor particularly poor. But while Will enjoyed a happy and comfortable childhood, his parents were strict with both him and his brother and sisters: Will would resent the discipline they imposed while he was growing up, but later apply it to his own children.

Will Smith would soon be transformed into that extremely rare phenomenon as both singer-songwriter and actor.

Will's father was an Air Force veteran who brought a military approach to the Smith family's home life. 'My father was a psychotic disciplinarian,' joked Will when discussing his strictly-controlled upbringing. 'It was a real military kind of house. There was a military type of structure and discipline.'

Willard senior tried to teach his kids clear lessons about how the world worked, about earning rewards – and how they had to try harder simply because they were from a black family. 'My parents planned "strategic wins" for all the children,' remembered Will, 'things that looked impossible that we were forced to do. My father is one of these guys who would do everything himself. He wouldn't call a plumber, wouldn't call for the dentist. You'd say, "Oh, Dad, I got a toothache." He'd say, "Oh, boy, go out to the truck and get my toolbox."'

'It's always been fun for me to tell a story and make people laugh. I've always been a show-off.'

Willard intended his children, especially Will and Harry, to grow up with a firm conviction that they could achieve anything that they turned their minds to. 'One year, he tore the brick front off the building, and my brother and I actually had to mix concrete by hand, then lay the bricks one at a time,' recalled Will. 'The wall was probably 50 feet wide and sixteen feet high. We thought it was impossible . . . I remember the day it was finished, six months later. We stood there and my father said, "Don't you ever tell me there's something you can't do." He'd been waiting six months to deliver that line. In my mind, it was instilled that anything you ever want to do, you do it one brick at a time.

'I remember standing there thinking, "There's no way I will live to see this completed." He wanted us to build the Great Wall of Philly! I remember hoping that my father would get committed, because if he were in an insane asylum, then we wouldn't have to finish the thing.'

Will was twelve and his brother Harry almost ten when their father taught them that invaluable lesson. Later, Will would appreciate the message that what seemed impossible was often achievable, a hard lesson but one which formed a philosophy of life for Will Smith. 'I got it: there's nothing insurmountable if you just keep laying the bricks, you know? You go one brick at a time and eventually there will be a wall. You can't avoid it. So, I don't worry too much about walls. I just concentrate on the bricks, and the walls take care of themselves.'

According to his parents, Will was quick to show off his performing talents at every opportunity, whether fooling around in the house or creating imaginative games to play with his brother and sisters. Family home movies focused on little Will, cheekily pulling faces for the camera, aware even then of how to make his presence felt on film. 'It's always been fun for me to tell a story and make people laugh. I've always been a show-off. I only got uncomfortable when people weren't looking at me,' he later admitted of the desire for attention that would feature throughout both his childhood and his adolescence.

Will's younger sister Ellen – who now works with her brother Harry in running Will's Los Angeles office – recalled growing up with a performing clown for an older brother. 'Will did the gross things kids do, like put straws up his nose,' she remembered. 'Will was punished first because he's older than me and Harry, and because he usually started things. Then he'd do something like make faces that would crack us up – and we'd end up getting punished worse.'

Younger brother Harry had a very different recollection of growing up in Will's shadow. 'He used to bum around everywhere, I always remember his feet used to stink. My mom would make him wash his feet.'

It was Will's grandmother, Helen Bright, who first turned his childish antics into serious performances. Casting her exuberant grandson in several church plays and pageants, she allowed young Will to take centre stage. 'My grandmother put us all in her little plays at Resurrection Baptist Church,' he remembered. Living nearby to the family, she was a strong influence on Will and an important part of the extended family, which, according to Willard Smith senior, featured 'two grandmothers, two great grandmothers and one great, great grandmother'. Grandmother Bright also used to organise the community Easter Egg hunts and arrange the holiday entertainment for the local neighbourhood kids.

Although not strongly religious, Will went to church with his extended family every Sunday. 'I don't believe in God as a person,' he later admitted. 'I don't believe God gets angry and zaps someone. I believe in the power of a higher being, that we can find our way into good graces or not. I believe positive energy begets positive energy, negative energy begets negative energy. It's less about punishment and reward, and more about attraction of what you project.'

Despite his New Age slant on religion, Will was raised to believe in an almighty creator. 'You have to believe in something greater than yourself,' he explained. 'You have to have faith in the power and believe it has your interests at heart. That's how I was raised by my parents, and that's the bottom line.' Whatever his own views were, the teaching of his parents remained very important to Will Smith.

On a cross country trip aged seven, Will was introduced to the true beauties of natural landscape. It was this experience that cemented his belief in a power greater than himself, if not in a supreme and vengeful God. 'We drove cross country and saw the natural wonders [of America], like Yellowstone National Park and the Grand Canyon,' remembered Will, vividly. 'We went to historical sites like Mt. Rushmore and the Alamo. When you see something beautiful, something bigger than you, whether created by nature or man, it changes you, it mellows you, it changes your attitude toward life.'

Like any young boy, Will loved sport. But he also had an interest in dinosaurs. He was also determined to be different from his fellow students and even claimed a liking for maths and science – the interest in science being purely a result of his

As The Fresh Prince of Bel-Air, *Will Smith had begun to make inroads into an acting career that he so desperately coveted.*

fascination for dinosaurs, of which he knew all the names (Stegosaurus being his favourite) and the details of the geological eras in which they lived. The certainty of science attracted the youngster: 'I guess they seemed definite, you know. Like something you could latch on to. A fact.'

His main interest, however, was music. Will had his first stereo system at ten years old, playing albums by Parliament, Funkadelic and the Bar-kays. Interested in developing what seemed to be natural musical abilities, he undertook piano lessons. The Smiths were a musical family: his father played the guitar, while his mother was not adverse to singing along. 'There were instruments around the house, and I just played a little of everything,' explained Will of his musical beginnings.

At the back of Will's early self-belief, as ever, was his family. 'Families are like a business, and the key is one person having a vision of what it needs to be and being able to pull everyone together and make it work,' he observed of his own family. 'It was always my mom, and my grandmom before her. Women are actually in charge of everything. The game of chess is the perfect example: where the king is kind of the figurehead but the queen is the most powerful piece on the board. Life is not unlike that.'

'When you see something beautiful, something bigger than you, whether created by nature or man, it changes you, it mellows you, it changes your attitude toward life.'

Will's mother, Caroline, claimed her son could talk before he could walk – a positive development for a future rapper. He was never happier as a toddler than when listening to the ridiculous rhymes of a Dr Seuss book. Will later jokingly claimed that it was Dr Seuss who first showed him the potential of rap: 'If you listen to them in a certain way, books like *Green Eggs and Ham* and *Hop on Pop* sound a lot like hip-hop.'

Caroline's influence was strongly felt in the choice of schooling for her children. While she was happy enough to encourage her eldest son's interest in musical performance, she tried to persuade him of the importance of a formal education in preparing for life in the real world. Part of her approach was to ensure that all her children spoke clear American English at home, banning any street slang from the house. To this day, Will maintains this attitude toward everyday language in his own household.

Will's education began at Our Lady of Lourdes Elementary School, a local, mostly white, Catholic school that he attended from kindergarten through to eighth grade, before switching to the mostly black Overbrook High. It would prove a useful foundation in learning how to appeal to diverse sections of the American public. 'I went to Catholic school for nine years and public school for three years, and that was the greatest education I could have had,' said Will. 'I went to school with all white people for nine years and then all black people for three years. Comedically, that helped me, because I have a great understanding of what black people think is funny and what white people think is funny. I'm able to find the joke that everyone thinks is hilarious, the record everyone thinks is moving, or a great dance record – walking that line where it's very specific to everyone, but universal at the same time.'

It is certain that these formative experiences helped to forge the key to international success. 'I think that transition is what helped me bridge the gap, because that's what my success has really been about: bridging the gap between the black community and the white community. Black people enjoy comedy about how the world is, while white people enjoy humour about how the world should be.'

At Our Lady of Lourdes, Will discovered an unexpected knack for storytelling and poetry which he decided to develop. This 'catholic' approach to life was also reflected in the social diversity of his area because although the Smith family belonged to the local Baptist church, he lived in a mainly black and Jewish community and often hung out with Muslim friends. These diverse influences taught him less about the differences between people than about their similarities, what brought them together rather than what drove them apart.

At school, Will was known more for his personal charm than for his academic achievements and quickly learned that his cheeky smile and quick wits allowed him to avoid all sorts of problems, including failure to deliver homework. Timekeeping was also a problem for young Will, who was constantly late for class but, despite this, he became known to teachers and students alike as 'Prince Charming', due to his ability to talk himself out of trouble. The tag caught on, and was soon abbreviated to just 'Prince'. After Will added the prefix 'Fresh', claiming he wanted to give his nickname 'that extra pizzazz', the title 'Fresh Prince' would remain with him long after his schooldays.

Will's clowning at elementary school was partly a compensation for what he felt he lacked in other departments. 'When I was little everybody always told me I looked like Alfred E. Neuman, the weird guy on the cover of *Mad Magazine*,' he has cheerfully admitted. 'I always had that square-looking hairdo, and I liked it, even though it made my ears stick out. One guy once told me that I looked like a car with the doors open.'

Smith's personal charm coupled with his cheeky smile and quick wits marked him out as one to watch.

Humour was, for him, a deliberate way of making friends and therefore avoiding the attention of bullies. It also put him centre stage, where he was happiest. Walking a fine line between entertaining his fellow students and getting into serious trouble with his teachers was often a problem, but fear of his parents kept him just the right side of that line. 'My father had so much control over me when I was growing up – I didn't have too much of an opportunity to do things the wrong way. He was always there to make sure I knew what the right way was.'

That awareness, however, never stopped Will getting up to teenage high jinks. At the age of fourteen he went for an ill-advised joyride in his father's truck, managing to collide with a car. Luckily for Will, the other driver was uninjured, uninsured and had no driver's license, so he quickly fled the scene. However, the minor damage to the truck meant Will had to face up to his father. 'My dad just grabbed my wrist and held it tightly, looked at me and said: "You'll never do that again, right?" and I said, "Right, dad."'

'There are individual personality traits of celebrities and sports stars and other people whom I admire, but the only people I ever idolised are my parents.'

As a teenager in the early eighties, Will Smith was always outgoing and energetic, determined to enjoy life despite his parents' focus on the importance of doing well at school. He never received particularly good grades, but always knew enough to get by. Given his aptitude for science and maths, his parents began to dream of a future for their son at Harvard or Massachusetts Institute of Technology, two of America's most prestigious colleges.

However, Will was not willing to think that far ahead. His philosophy was living for the here and now, almost as a reckless counter-reaction to his father's military discipline and his mother's concern about education. 'I would have been the attention-deficit hyperactive-disorder poster child,' he later recalled of his schooldays.

Aware of both his musical abilities and talents as the class clown who could get away with anything ('I would talk to someone and get them into trouble,' he gleefully told Oprah Winfrey), Will did have dreams of making it big and emulating some of his heroes. Mostly these idols were local Philadelphia sports stars, like basketball greats Wilt Chamberlain and Julius 'Dr J' Erving, as well as Philadelphia-born NASA astronaut Guion Bluford.

'The first person I looked up to, admired and said "I want to be like that person" was Julius Erving,' recalled Will. 'I remember taking note of how well he expressed himself when someone put the camera or microphone in front of him . . . calm and poised. He always had something interesting to say, and he said it well. I remember thinking, "I want to speak that way."'

Other role models during his teenage years included TV star Bill Cosby and, especially, comedian/movie star Eddie Murphy, who he saw as breaking down the barriers to success in the white-dominated American entertainment industry. However, his admiration of superstar millionaires was not young Will's main driving force – that was his own family. 'There are individual personality traits of celebrities and sports stars and other people whom I admire, but the only people I ever idolised are my parents,' he admitted. This strength of self-belief that his background gave young Will allowed him to entertain ambitions far beyond the ordinary: 'I wasn't the kind of kid who dreamed about being a fireman or a policeman. I wanted to go up in the space shuttle.'

The musical climate in America during the early eighties was changing. Will was quick to pick up on the growing popularity of rap, which was developing from a street culture into a broader-based form of entertainment. 'As an urban kid, I picked up on rap,' he noted of how he found his first springboard to international fame. Back in 1979, aged just eleven, Will heard 'Rapper's Delight' by the Sugar Hill Gang on the radio. Mindful of his own rhyming and musical talents, he was struck by a motivating thought: 'They weren't doing anything I couldn't do. I could put words together well and get a point across with lyrics. It's a natural skill . . .'

Will Smith's first rap audience consisted of his immediate family, his fellow Philadelphia teens whom he entertained at local parties, his school friends who joined in as he rapped between classes, and even passers-by who were entertained by the Fresh Prince practising his new-found skills on street corners at weekends.

The Sugar Hill Gang had much to answer for. 'I started rapping just as soon as I heard that first song. I rapped all day long, until I thought my mom was going to lose her mind! Music, after all, has always been in my heart. At first, I did it as a hobby, and I enjoyed it and got really good at it.'

As part of rap's street-culture legacy, deprivation, crime and drugs were fast becoming prime subject matter for many rap artists. But although he got into the music, his father's warnings were strong enough to deter Will from the downside of the urban rap experience. 'There were a lot of nights when I was in the wrong place with the wrong people at the wrong time,' he recalled of his street-level experiences. 'There were situations where, if one thing goes bad, you could end up in jail or dead.'

Aware his son was moving in potentially dangerous territory, Willard Smith took him for a drive through some of Philadelphia's more notorious neighbourhoods as an object lesson on the dangers of the lifestyle increasingly associated with rap music. 'He pointed to the bums sleeping in the doorways and said: "This is what people look like when they do drugs,"' remembered Will.

It was a salutary lesson, but only the latest in a long line of stern lesssons handed out by his father. 'I hated being in trouble,' Will admitted much later. 'I was so petrified of my parents that I managed to avoid most of the pitfalls that teens fall in. I just knew when I went to school that if a teacher had to call home, my life was on the line. My father was a serious disciplinarian. I wouldn't dare bring home a "D" on my report card. The bottom line was no nonsense. I can remember probably five times in my life when my father hit me, because he never really had to. I was so petrified.'

'When you enjoy what you do, you're gonna get good at it.'

Fear of his father's reaction kept the teenage Will Smith away from drugs. 'He did his shaping up by taking little chunks out of your behind,' said Will of his father's physical punishment for wrong-doing. 'There was no peer pressure [to do drugs] that was strong enough to make it worth dealing with my father. He wanted to make sure that I knew that he was my biggest, strongest peer influence.'

Of his father's positive influence, Will later claimed: 'What my father always made clear to me is to just do one thing well. If you do one thing well, everything else will come from that. I started off rapping and really concentrated on that – then the television show came from that and I worked really hard, and the next thing you know, I'm doing movies. When you enjoy what you do, you're gonna get good at it.'

Despite their faith in the family, the marriage between Willard Smith and his wife Caroline did not last. They separated when Will was aged thirteen. 'My parents were very loving,' recalled their eldest son, who has long refused to discuss the details of his parents' break-up. 'We never felt like our parents didn't love us. No matter how difficult things got or how angry someone may have gotten, no matter what happened in our lives, we always felt that we had somewhere to go.'

Will seems to have taken a remarkably mature approach to his parents' separation. 'It really didn't bother me,' he claimed. 'I was extremely precocious and realised that my parents were much better off being apart. It brought peace to the house and each parent. My mother moved in with her mother, and we all spent weekends together. Our family remained close-knit, except my parents never talked to each other!'

It was also at the age of thirteen that Will Smith took his first awkward steps toward sexual experience, the teenage obsession that had all his classmates in its grip. While his mother was picking up his brother and sister from school, Will invited his then-girlfriend Ramona down to the laundry room of his house. As he and Ramona had been friends for over a year and had 'grown up', reaching the giddy heights of the eighth grade, Will decided it was time to see just how mature they really were. Responsible as ever, young Will took a trip to the local corner store to buy condoms from Mr Bryant, the friendly local storekeeper. Bryant simply gave Will a stern look and handed over the contraceptives free of charge. 'The look said everything,' remembered Will clearly, the event having carved a permanent place in his memory. 'It was kind of like: You're doing the right thing by being safe and smart, but you really don't need to be doing it anyway.'

From there, Will's would-be romantic liaison went rapidly downhill. The laundry room was not the most romantic of settings, with he and Ramona lying on piles of dirty clothing. Adding to his problems, Will could not get the condom packet open, then dropped the condom, surprised at how slippery it was. There seemed to be so many obstacles in their way that Will and Ramona gave up, their passion having long since faded.

It would be almost three years before a fifteen-year-old Will finally lost his virginity to a girl called Gina in 1984. This time, in a more comfortable part of the basement, everything was planned like a military operation – a lesson doubtless learned from his father, and his previous experience with Ramona. This time Will was successful, so much so that he and Gina would continue to see each other, on and off, for the next four years.

It was no surprise that, given his close ties with his mother, Will decided to live mostly with Caroline after his parents divorced. He continued to work for his father after school in the refrigeration business, but their relationship was a complex and difficult one, full of fear and competition in equal measure. Willard had begun to teach Will how to play chess at the age of eight – a game he has always loved, intending to teach it to Trey, his own son. However, shortly after the divorce, when Will was fourteen, he was finally able to beat his father at a game. It was a significant moment for them both. 'I saw the checkmate coming,' remembers Will, 'and I was petrified.' However, in his defeat Willard saw another milestone in his son's growth. 'It built my self-esteem,' confirmed the actor of this rite-of-passage.

It was from his father's domineering influence that Will Smith inherited his strong work ethic. By example, Willard Smith senior had shown his son what it meant to work – even when you didn't enjoy what you were doing.

'My father was a man who could do some work,' Will asserted. 'We would do installations, put these big freezer cases in supermarkets. A lot of the time, we ended up working in the basement – the nastiest place you could ever be in. One time we were in this place, and there was like two inches of muddy thick old food gunk on the floor and there was a big old dead rat. My father, with his bare hands, picked up the dead rat and threw it out of the way. Then he put his head down on the floor, right where the rat had been, and went to work. And he never flinched, you know?'

While Will knows his career will never be 'hard work' in the sense that his father's was, he thanks his father for the get-the-job-done-well attitude he inherited. 'What I do is difficult sometimes,' he admits, 'but what my father did was real work. I never complain at work. No matter how difficult it is, no matter how much of an asshole the person is that I'm working with, no matter how hot, no matter how shitty the day is. I see a lot of people complaining – I thank God everyday that I don't have to feed my family shovin' rats out of the way and putting my head on a nasty floor under a compressor. There are much worse jobs to have than this.'

Work ethic aside, it was Will Smith's fascination with rap music that absorbed his attention during his late teenage years, serving as it did as an escape from the pressures of family life, demands that he succeed at school, and the failure of his parents' marriage. Soon Will was gaining a reputation as a local talent, a whiz with words who could more than hold his own in any of the on-the-street rapping competitions that spontaneously sprang up. 'My reputation came from beating other rappers in street challenges. I never lost a street battle,' claimed Will. 'I was going to all these block parties, having fun and competing with my raps. It suddenly occurred to me, "Okay, if I'm going to party, I might as well get paid for it . . ."'

Since the age of thirteen, Will Smith had earned money as a neighbourhood house-party DJ. Apart from the usual DJ spiel, it was a very different style to rapping – but Will soon merged the two in his own unique way. Unable to contain himself after his first few gigs, Will began rapping between records and building up a solid reputation for himself.

The mainstream popularity of rap was growing in early-to-mid-eighties America. Will, then listening to records by Crash Crew, Kurtis Blow and the Cold Crush Brothers, was convinced he could make a similar mark. The time had come to become a full-blown rap act and gain a record deal.

It was a big step, and it was not something Will formally announced to his parents. They were still hoping their son would achieve the school grades to enable him to go to college. The computer industry was taking off at the time, and his father had suggested a future for Will as a computer engineer. Will said nothing about his musical ambitions, but quietly formed a rap duo with his school friend Clarence 'Clate' Holmes, who adopted the rap name Ready Rock-C. They performed at local events, with Will writing the songs and performing as the Fresh Prince.

Smith proved to be a natural performer on the stage, a quality he would soon use to good effect in his burgeoning acting career.

Convinced they could go professional, Will and Clarence approached well-known rap producer Dana Goodman with a bunch of Will's songs. Impressed though he was, Goodman nonetheless sent the hopeful duo away, advising them to develop a lot more material before approaching anyone again. It was a blow to Will's professional hopes – but salvation was around the corner in the form of Jeff Townes, a Philadelphia rapper known to everyone in the area as DJ Jazzy Jeff.

'People I went to school with probably remember me as a jackass.'

Townes was from southwest Philadelphia, growing up not far from Will. Two years older than Will, Jeff had a head start on a professional music career. Captivated by 'scratching' – mixing elements of different records together – Jeff had secured an outlet for his talents on a local Philadelphia radio station. By 1983, then aged seventeen, DJ Jazzy Jeff was one of the top names in the local rap talent pool, and had even released a single on a local record label (although it flopped).

The fateful meeting between the Fresh Prince and Jazzy Jeff took place in January 1984 at a block party in Will's area. Will was just sixteen, with plenty of experience but lacking in the professional recognition Jeff had enjoyed for years. 'I had heard of Will,' said Townes, 'but I already had someone that I worked with. When I played that party on Will's block, naturally he was there. He asked if he could rap for a while – and it was like natural chemistry. He flowed with what I did and I flowed with exactly what he did, and we knew it. We just clicked the whole night long.'

From the beginning, Will and Jeff took a distinctive approach to rap music – partly due to their upbringings, but also on account of their desire just to have fun. Their brand of rap was humorous, clean, almost family-oriented. It was an approach that led to them – with Will's pal and previous rapping partner Ready Rock-C on the beatbox – being asked to play church halls and kids' parties as well as night-clubs. 'We had a pretty new style that people were finding interesting,' noted Will of their light-hearted rap songs, 'plus, we could make people laugh at a party scene.'

One influence on Will's family-friendly approach was his grandmother, Helen Bright. When he first started writing rap lyrics, aged twelve, he kept a notebook full of lyrical ideas very much in the style of the rap music he was hearing around him – in what he himself might have termed 'full bodied' language. His grandmother disliked what she read when she found the notebook one day, adding a little note for her grandson: 'Dear Will, Truly intelligent people do not have to use this type of language to express themselves. Why don't you show the world that you are as smart as we all think you are?' Her honesty struck a chord with young Will: he decided that if his songs were ever to be played on the radio, he wanted his family – and grandmother Helen, in particular – to be proud of what they heard.

He may have started to enjoy some success on the local rap scene, but Will Smith was still only sixteen. His parents insisted that a satisfactory conclusion to his education was required, before he could take his musical 'hobby' any more seriously. From ninth grade onwards Will had studied at Overbrook High School, but had no real interest in schoolwork now that his musical endeavours were taking off. 'I was just silly all the time,' he sheepishly admits of his later school days. 'People I went to school with probably remember me as a jackass.'

Despite his lack of interest in all things academic, Will still found it easy to get decent – if not spectacular – grades. 'I got the grades mainly to please my parents,' he admitted. 'I didn't think I'd ever use what I learned. But in my rap and as an actor, it's amazing how much of what I did learn comes back to me. It all pays off in the end, I just didn't know it then.'

After playing a few local house parties together, Will Smith and Jeff Townes began to get bigger ideas. Will was particularly keen to rectify his previous failure to secure a record deal. According to Jeff, he felt much more confident second time around: 'We were laughing and joking like we'd known each other for ten years,' he noted, as the pair formulated their masterplan. 'Together we could be the ultimate – not just in Philadelphia, but everywhere. Nobody could touch us.'

02

EVERYTHING THAT GLITTERS AIN'T ALWAYS GOLD

When Will Smith reached the end of his high school years, he was faced with a difficult choice. He had worked hard at school to maintain his grades, simply in order to keep his parents happy. With their encouragement, he had won a scholarship to study at the Massachusetts Institute of Technology, one of America's most prestigious colleges. Will's mother and father were overjoyed, but he was none too happy at this unexpected turn of events.

During 1985, a local small-time record producer had approached Will Smith and Jeff Townes – then wowing the Philadelphia rap scene as the Fresh Prince and DJ Jazzy Jeff – about cutting a single for the local club scene. Dana Goodman, who had sent Will away several years previously, had hooked the duo up with independent outfit Word Records. Jumping at the chance, despite doubts about the viability of the operation (Will remembers the 'producer' was operating from the trunk of his car), Will and Jeff prepared to record their first professional track.

Will with his partner Jeff Townes. Together, as the Fresh Prince and DJ Jazzy Jeff, they would achieve rewards beyond their wildest dreams.

This was what Will really wanted to do.

The track was an early version of their first international hit single, 'Girls Ain't Nothing But Trouble', which quickly became popular on the Philadelphia club scene, and secured radio play on local R'n'B and rap stations. This was what Will had been hoping for ever since he and Clarence Holmes tried to secure a record deal – but greater success was to come. Will and Jeff were contacted by Jive Records, a company with a better distribution network, who offered them $15,000 each to buy the rights to the single for nation-wide release across the USA.

This was an entirely different career path to the one his parents expected Will to travel on. 'He was going to be a computer engineer,' said Caroline of her son's prospects. 'Him as a rapper was definitely not what I had in mind.'

'She had a conniption,' was how Will described his mother's reaction. Will's father was more relaxed about his son's new direction, seeing as how Will was applying himself in the way he had been taught. As there was one final year of school left before Will was supposed to start college, Willard Smith decided to give his son a chance to prove himself. 'My mother let me talk to my father,' recalled Will. 'He was none too thrilled with the course of events, but my father basically said, "Okay, take a year. If it works, God bless you. If it doesn't, you'll go to college."'

'We're trying to show the world, that you can dress nicely and speak well and still be considered black.'

It was all the time Will needed. 'Girls Ain't Nothing but Trouble' – a twelve-inch single about the perils of teen romance – stood out from the standard hard-edged rap songs of NWA and Public Enemy. It was not only a big seller in the US, but proved phenomenally popular in Britain and soon clocked up sales in excess of 100,000 copies. Will Smith was on his way to the top.

Despite all this, Will found it hard to take his overnight fame seriously. After all, he was still ploughing away at school to make sure his math grades were high enough to please his parents. One hit record would not be enough to convince his father he was justified in passing up a place at Massachusetts Institute of Technology. 'It was fun,' said Will of the summer of 1986, when his first single was breaking. 'I thought if these people are foolish enough to pay me for something I was going to do anyway, then okay.'

During the summer break from school, Will and Jeff went on their first concert tour. Playing on the DefJam tour, support to major rap stars like LL Cool J, Eric B. & Rakim, Whodini and Public Enemy, it was a real taste of the lifestyle they aspired to. However, it was only when DJ Jazzy Jeff and the Fresh Prince reached London that they became aware of their growing teenage following. Getting off the plane at Heathrow Airport, Will was surprised at their reception. 'There were screaming girls at the airport, and we thought "What is this? What are they screaming for?"'

The adulation was welcome – Will was just a teenager himself, although he had reached his adult height of six foot three inches, while Jeff had been working at a rap career for close on ten years. Less pleasurable was the criticism that followed rapidly on the heels of acclaim. Other rappers saw Will's family-friendly lyrics and the pair's sense of humour as a betrayal of 'real' rap, while the music press criticised 'Girls Ain't Nothing but Trouble' for sexism.

'That's a ridiculous, idiotic opinion,' fumed Will at the time. 'The rap is a personal story, told with a sense of humour, rather than a statement of general attitude.' As if in answer to the criticism, however, he and Jeff recorded a counter-track with a female rapper called 'Guys Ain't Nothing but Trouble'. The other criticism, that the pair were peddling 'soft' rap, would dog their success for the next few years. As far as Will was concerned, he was never uncomfortable with the commerciality of his work – popularity and success were 'for him' the whole point of embarking on a showbusiness career.

Will was happy to produce family-friendly rap. Still, he refused to blame hardcore or gangsta rap for the incidents of crime and violence so often associated with the music. 'People are responsible for their own actions,' he claimed. 'There was a case [in Texas] where this kid was trying to say a Tupac [Shakur] record made him shoot a police officer. That is the most ridiculous assertion I've ever heard in my life. A record can't make you do anything. I can relate to the emotion. I remember being young and coming out of a Bruce Lee movie and being hyped. We're jumping around and kicking each other, but a Bruce Lee movie can't make me get into a fight. We, as individuals, have to take responsibilities for our actions.'

The next step was to follow up the unexpected success of the single by producing an album. Early in 1987, the duo came out with *Rock the House* – featuring the talents of 'human beatbox' Ready Rock-C, Will paying his dues to a friend who helped his dreams of a musical career become a reality. This light-hearted, upbeat album made Will stand out from the massed ranks of angry, downbeat rappers, quickly selling 600,000 copies and qualifying as a gold record. It was enough to prove to Will that the success of the first record had not been a one-off lucky accident.

It was also enough for Will's father to finally give up hope of persuading his son to pursue higher education. Despite his parents' disappointment, they were keen for Will to follow the course he was determined to take – as long as he took the rough with the smooth and learned his lessons as he went along.

Will Smith was getting an education, but it was in showbusiness rather than in high school. After graduating, the eighteen-year-old threw himself into developing material for a second album with Jazzy Jeff. This would take eighteen months of hard work, but in the meantime he had to become used to fame, not only in Philadelphia, but across the world.

The second album built upon the strengths of the first, fulfilling all its promise. DJ Jazzy Jeff and the Fresh Prince were clearly not going to be one-hit wonders. Released in 1988, *He's the DJ, I'm the Rapper* was a double album, unusual at the time for rappers. More commercially popular than their first, it clearly showed how Will and Jeff had worked at their craft. The songs still dealt with personal concerns in a light, humorous way – often reflecting their own experiences, as on 'Here We Go Again' – but they also showed a distinct inventiveness in their musical style and approach. Will sang about dating on 'Let's Get Busy Baby', while Jeff was able to pay tribute to his favourite horror film, Wes Craven's *A Nightmare on Elm Street,* on the track 'Nightmare on My Street'.

The obvious single on the album, 'Parents Just Don't Understand', dealt with the horrors of teenagers going shopping for clothes with their highly unfashionable mothers. A fast-paced, funny video which featured heavily on MTV made the single a hit, and the album went on to sell three million copies in its first few months of release.

The commercial success of the second album did not silence the critics who felt Will Smith had betrayed rap. If the songs were not hard-hitting stories about drugs and deprivation or life on the streets, then it wasn't 'real'. One attack in particular, from rapper Big Daddy Kane, stung Will. Kane accused him of producing music purely to appeal to a white audience, far removed from the roots of rap music.

'I don't think anybody can dictate what's black and what's not black,' responded Will in an interview with *USA Today*. 'Big Daddy Kane is ignorant and doesn't realise what black really means. He thinks being articulate is being white. We're trying to show the world, and black kids, that you can dress nicely and speak well and still be considered black. Our music is black music. Our families are black, we came from black backgrounds.'

Will was determined to show that his own suburban background was just as 'real' as that of any deprived urban rap artist, and that he had just as much right

The Fresh Prince at the American Music Awards.

to self-expression as anyone else. He refused to take the criticisms personally, but equally refused to accept that appealing to a bigger audience, whether black or white, was any kind of failing.

'We're going to continue to rap about things we have experienced,' Will said of himself and Jeff Townes. 'Not only that, but lots of people can relate to us. In "Parents Just Don't Understand", we wanted to write about something everybody could relate to. I wasn't trying to appeal to a white audience, I was writing about what I related to, what I thought was interesting'.

Another bone of contention for older rappers was DJ Jazzy Jeff and the Prince's sense of fun and lack of seriousness. The fact that their videos, which played frequently on MTV, were funny – often at the expense of Will and Jeff themselves – was seen as somehow contrary to the spirit of rap. 'We are humorous,' admitted Will at the time, 'we like to have fun. We let our personalities run through our work. Both of us have a good sense of humour and we don't act any differently when we make a record. I don't understand groups who come on stage looking real mad. We just want people to have fun. You don't have to come on rough to rap.'

The ultimate response to this critical carping was for Will Smith and Jeff Townes to scoop up Best Rap Album and Best Rap Artists awards at the National Music Awards in January 1989. Arriving home for a celebration dinner, Will was brought back down to earth when Jeff's mother insisted on sending her son and his friend out to buy groceries. The award-winning rap stars, could not leave real-life behind, no matter how big they were getting.

When 'Parents Just Don't Understand' made history by winning the first ever Grammy Award for Rap the following month, Will and Jeff refused to turn up to accept their unique award. The Grammies were more prestigious than the National Music Awards, voted for by music business insiders rather than based on sales and airplay. Apparently, however, the duo had become politicised when fighting their corner against other rappers – when they discovered the rap award had been grouped with the 'less mainstream' technical prizes, rather than the rest of the popular music awards, the duo refused to accept their prize. At the following year's awards ceremony the Grammy committee were forced to include the rap category as part of the mainstream show. The duo's stance had made a difference – their stand had been taken on behalf of rap as a musical genre that should be heard and enjoyed by as wide an audience as possible.

While Will's musical success was born of his own talent and determination, there was also a hefty dose of simply being-in-the-right-place-at-the-right-time. Rap was becoming mainstream in the late eighties, crossing over from black urban audiences to white suburbia, and Will was at the forefront of the change. He both drove it forward and reaped the rewards, and has continued to be one of its main beneficiaries throughout the 1990's. 'The bottom line,' he admitted, 'is that rap is generating the most money of any form of music right now. The music is good, realistic. Mainstream businessmen and the industry are opening up.'

With success for Will Smith came money – and all the benefits and problems associated with it. The unexpected success of DJ Jazzy Jeff and the Prince resulted in an unimaginable windfall, which teenager Will was not ready to cope with. With the same short-term attitude he had displayed at school and while making his first records, Will decided it was time he and Jeff started 'livin' large'.

They immediately hired many of their friends and acquaintances from Philadelphia as roadies, bodyguards and dancers to go on the promotional tour for *He's the DJ, I'm the Rapper*. Whenever they had to travel, they travelled by hired limousine. Eating out was less of an event, more of an everyday occurrence – but only at the priciest restaurants they could find.

'Music was always a casual thing, a hobby. But it took off. By the time I was eighteen, I had two million dollars and eight cars in the garage.'

Will's parents watched the changes in their son warily. As well as the profligate personal spending, he was providing for his family, so their criticisms of his expenditure and lifestyle were muted at first. Caroline simply hoped that the novelty of the windfall would wear off, and the smart, responsible Will would return to make some prudent investments.

As far as Will was concerned, that was not going to happen anytime soon. He was having the time of his life. Faced with the option of behaving responsibly, or even studying at MIT, he preferred to be partying long and hard and hanging out at Hollywood parties where he met his idols, such as Eddie Murphy.

Will felt fully justified in spending the cash as it rolled in. Record sales followed an upward slant, while an innovative phone line that played recorded messages from Jazzy Jeff and the Fresh Prince brought in more money than all the record sales combined, receiving over two million calls in the first six months of operation. In the year 1989-90, the phone line alone grossed ten million dollars. With that kind of gold mine, why would Will consider curtailing his spending?

Looking back at that period in his life, Will believes his attitude to money was a disaster just waiting to happen. 'I had the suburban mansion, a motorcycle, I was travelling around the world,' he remembered of his first flush of success. 'I was eighteen and the world was open and when the world is open like that it makes you crazy, you want everything.'

'Success hasn't changed me. Now, the difference is I can get two burgers instead of one.'

By the time of his eighteenth birthday, Will Smith was a millionaire several times over and determined to let everyone know it. 'I never had a big plan,' admitted Will candidly. 'Music was always a casual thing, a hobby. But it took off. By the time I was eighteen, I had two million dollars and eight cars in the garage.'

The cars were status symbols – Will was simply an average American teenager, taking things to the materialistic extreme because he was capable of doing so. In the garages of his five-bedroom mansion in Merion, an exclusive suburb of Philadelphia, Will stashed a Corvette, a bright red Camaro (which he bought as soon as he received his first $15,000 from Jive Records for 'Girls Ain't Nothing But Trouble'), a truck, a Suburban Station Wagon and a Suzuki bike. Of course, all Will's cars came with a state-of-the-art stereo system attached.

The mansion became home to Will and brother Harry. Reflecting their age group, it featured a large pool room and a basketball hoop as the centrepiece of the living room, a hot tub built into the master bedroom, and a kitchen large enough to be described as 'a mini-mart'.

In 1987 *Rock the House* had gone gold, while 1988's *He's the DJ, I'm the Rapper* sold three million copies, spurred by the success of 'Parents Just Don't Understand'. Another record was needed to keep the income flowing in, if not to provide Will and Jeff with a creative outlet. Music seemed to have taken a back seat to spending and indulgence. Their 'livin' large' attitude even affected the recording of the third album, released as *And in This Corner* in 1989. Will and Jeff decided they could now afford to do it in style, flying to the Bahamas resort of Compass Point. They rented the beachside villa of rock star Robert Palmer, brought most of the Philadelphia posse with them and set about trying to work.

By the time he was eighteen, Smith was a millionaire several times over.

The distractions of sun, sand, sea and sex got in the way and, at the end of their allotted two weeks, only four tracks had been laid down for the new album.

Not that it worried Will – excess and the rock-star lifestyle go together, after all. He refused to recognise that he was acting out of character, despite warnings from

Will Smith livin' it large, but he would soon realise that fame and fortune carried some stiff penalties.

his parents. 'I'm pretty much the same person,' Will protested at the time. 'Success hasn't changed me. Now, the difference is I can get two burgers instead of one.'

Shopping became an extravagant addiction, while Will had no-one to seriously advise him on handling his money. 'One year I spent $800,000,' he sheepishly admitted. 'I went through it so fast it made my head spin. I had a problem. Whenever I got a little bored, I'd go shopping. At least I bought my mother a house. I realised I had to change my attitude. Now, instead of getting bored, I put that energy into my work.'

During 1988 and 1989, the combination of inexperience, youth, arrogance and affluence drove Will Smith to extremes. 'Once I flew to London and Tokyo, just to buy clothes,' he claimed. On another occasion, Will and his gang of hangers-on flew to Atlanta and insisted that the local Gucci store was closed to the public to allow him exclusive access. The shop co-operated, knowing that they had a customer to whom money was no object. The trip was all the more bizarre as there was a Gucci store in Atlantic City, less than one hour's drive from Philadelphia. That was too mundane for Will, however, who got a thrill from flying somewhere unknown to him simply to go shopping. 'It was a power trip,' the star later admitted.

Will took to gambling, in Las Vegas and Atlantic City, with friendly wagers of several thousand dollars not an unusual occurrence. He also bought copious amounts of jewellery, including an ostentatious gold necklace which spelled out the name 'Fresh Prince' in diamonds. In retrospect, Will's extravagance seems amusing, but the actor insists otherwise. 'There was nothing funny about it,' he said of his youthful indulgences. 'It was a matter of being young, wild and stupid. But there was nothing anyone could have done. At that age, with that amount of money, it's difficult to handle. And because I was eighteen, the cheques came to me. So it was difficult for anyone to intervene in the ludicrous behaviour I was displaying. Besides, I didn't listen to anyone. Everything my parents taught me went out the window as soon as that cash hit the bank account.'

Will's mother continued to plead with her son, urging him to avoid the temptations of drugs and cut out the fast driving which was attracting the attention of the police. His father was more scathing of his son's largesse. 'He saw me blowing money that could allow me to set myself up for the rest of my life,' said Will. When his son bragged about the six cars and two motorbikes he owned, Willard senior snapped back: 'What do you need six cars for when you only have one butt?'

It was the fast cars which brought Will face-to-face with the institutionalised racism of the police force, his stardom offering no immunity. 'In the two years I had my Corvette, I probably got stopped 35 or 40 times,' he claimed. 'At least five to ten of those times, I was told I was stopped because "We want to know where you got this car?" A young black guy with a nice car is going to get stopped, period. And the cops will tell you that.'

Will's problems with the police did not stop at his cars. 'I had an experience in Philadelphia, asking a cop why he'd stopped me. He said: "Because you're a fucking nigger" and spat in my car. I've been punched in the face and kicked by police. Fill out a report and internal affairs will say, basically, that what you said didn't happen. All through life growing up as a young black man, you see that happen to everybody around you. The cops killing someone and getting away with it. So probably from the time that you can understand race, seven or eight years old, there's a weight that you carry. If a white person gets into a fight with a black guy, he feels safer when the cops come. For the black guy, now you're really scared, because you've won the first fight, but now there's a guy with a gun and a nightstick.'

'Even now, driving – I know I'm Will Smith and I have money and I live in a nice neighbourhood, but the police are street soldiers who are specifically sent out to destroy me because of the colour of my skin.'

Racism was not limited to the forces of law and order. Will vividly recalls taking his first-class seat for an aeroplane flight, only to be challenged by the flight attendant who demanded to see his ticket. His parents had brought Will up to expect and to deal with racism, but he had believed that somehow his wealth and fame would make things different. He was rapidly discovering that his money did not buy special treatment, nor did it necessarily bring greater happiness.

'By 1989, I was broke. When the money ran out, so did my so-called friends. That was a big lesson.'

'I wasn't any happier with money,' claimed Will, despite the travel, houses, cars, clothes and all his other possessions. 'I wasn't any less happy when I went broke. I spent a lot of money – then it becomes difficult to handle. I would blow my cheques as soon as I received them, and I was so arrogant and stupid in those days that I refused to listen to any advice anyone gave me on how to properly manage my money.'

As quickly as it started, the cash flow ceased as the IRS (Internal Revenue Service, the American tax-collecting body) realised that Will Smith was due to pay a huge tax bill on his sudden earnings. No provision had been made for this, and Will found his assets frozen after less than a year of 'livin' large'.

'In 1987-1988 I was rich,' he said, wearily. 'In 1989 I was broke. There's nothing more sobering than having six cars and a mansion one day, and you can't even buy gas for the cars the next. I was broke, like sell-the-car broke. Actually, you know what? Sell-everything broke. I was a moron. It hurt, and mentally it was tough dealing with it, but inside it didn't change. I still had my family, and I could still have a good time. I could still laugh.'

The shock of losing everything was not the only bad news. As soon as the tax man came calling, Will's posse – those friends, acquaintances and hangers-on whose way he had been paying for the past year – quickly abandoned him, disappearing as fast as the cash. 'My fair weather friends helped me spend all my money,' he reflected. 'By 1989, I was broke. When the money ran out, so did my so-called friends. That was a big lesson.'

'My parents and my upbringing weighed out over the temptations of the glitter, the money, and all that. Who I really am wins every time.'

When the new album – *And in This Corner*, featuring the song 'I Think I Can Beat Mike Tyson' – only managed to scrape its way to gold disc status, some music critics said the days of DJ Jazzy Jeff and the Fresh Prince were numbered. Their family-friendly novelty rap act had finally worn thin.

'I had to grow up quickly,' Will admitted to the *New York Daily News*, as he faced his mounting financial problems. 'But in a way, I'm glad it happened. In life there are two types of people: those who make mistakes, and keep making the same mistakes over and over again, and those who learn from their mistakes. I like to think I'm the latter.'

This sudden, dramatic fall from grace brought Will to his senses very quickly. He realised he had lost sight of the principles which his parents had taught him to live by. He was determined to get himself back on top again, but to do it right this time. 'I had a period in my life where I sought attention,' Will later reflected. 'I had a little money and wanted to flex it all. But the real person inside me eventually dictated how I had to act, how I had to behave, and how I had to treat people. My parents and my upbringing weighed out over the temptations of the glitter, the money, and all that. Who I really am wins every time.'

Will recalled his father's advice about focus and concentration in terms of career goals. He set about planning a new career, one that would leave rap music behind for acting: as the lead character in the hit TV sitcom *The Fresh Prince of Bel-Air*. 'I always knew that there would be the next thing,' claimed Will, 'and I'm just glad the show came up when it did. It was perfect timing.'

03

TWINKLE, TWINKLE (I'M NOT A STAR)

The hit American sitcom *The Fresh Prince of Bel-Air* would not only provide the solution to Will Smith's financial problems, but would launch him on the road to stardom.

According to Jeff Townes, Will had always expressed an interest in a career as an actor as well as that of rap star – neither believed the transfer would be easy though. His work on their music videos had shown he was comfortable in front of the camera, and the high number of screenings on MTV had made his face very familiar to younger audiences.

The audience appeal of his Fresh Prince persona had not been overlooked by casting directors in Hollywood. Will and Jeff had even been offered the leading roles in a film: *House Party* (1990), directed by Reginald Hudlin.

A comedy about a group of urban black teenagers preparing for a party, the film seemed to be right up Will's alley, strongly reflecting his own background and music business success. That, though, was the problem – *House Party*, although giving Will the chance to act, would not have been a sufficient departure from his own life thus far. After giving the offer serious thought, Will and Jeff turned it down.

The focus on rap music in *House Party* had put Will and Jeff off, allowing rappers Kid 'n' Play to play the parts as a sly take-off of DJ Jazzy Jeff and the Fresh Prince. (Also in the cast was TV comedy star Martin Lawrence, who would go on to co-star with Will in the action-packed cop movie *Bad Boys* [1995]).

Will's switch to acting in 1990 was driven by more than just ambition – he had debts to pay, mainly to the IRS. It was also becoming clear that with the lower sales of *And in This Corner*, he could not rely solely on music to dig him out of a financial hole. It was a comedown for the cocky teenager who, just one year before, had earned over one million dollars. The dawn of the 1990's saw a more serious, responsible and sober Will Smith emerge from the excesses of the previous decade.

'In 1990 I was dealing with a decline in my music – at least in my eyes,' recalled Will. 'I was looking for something new, something else to do.' With the Internal Revenue Service breathing down his neck, it was important that Will Smith turn up that 'something else' quickly.

Still aged just 21, Will decided he would pursue acting seriously. An acting career was not the kind of thing he could make a success of in Philadelphia. Will broke the news to Jeff Townes that he intended a move to Hollywood. Jeff decided to remain in Philly, but the pair pledged to continue to work together. Will, never one to burn his bridges, was determined to keep his music career open in case his acting endeavours should fail.

Relocated to Los Angeles, Will was determined to use the fame left over from his musical success to open doors. Even when acting opportunities were laid before him, however, he was hesitant about taking the plunge. 'About a year before *The Fresh Prince*, I had a couple of opportunities to read for stuff on *The Cosby Show*, but I never had the heart to do it,' he lamented. As so often in Hollywood, Will's big break came from a chance meeting and the spark of an offbeat idea, leading to six years at the top of the television prime-time ratings league.

Benny Medina, a black record executive, was ten years older than Will Smith in 1990. He was vice-president in charge of the Black Music division at Warner Brothers and well aware of Jazzy Jeff and the Fresh Prince's phenomenal success. He related to their story of coming out of nowhere to make it in the music business, because he shared similar origins.

Medina had grown up in the infamous Watts district of East LA, known for its large, poor, black population, gang violence and drug problems. After his father disappeared during Benny's childhood, tragedy struck when his mother died and there were no relatives able or willing to take the young boy in. The rest of his early years were spent shuffling from pillar to post in the institutional child-care system, from juvenile centres to foster homes and back again.

At the age of fifteen, life changed for Benny Medina. He moved in with a new white foster family – that of Jack Elliot, a well-respected composer for television and films who counted Hollywood 'Rat Pack' members Frank Sinatra and Dean Martin among his friends, as well as Motown Records founder Berry Gordy. Elliot was also one of a number of showbusiness figures who sponsored the juvenile centre where Benny had been living previously. 'I literally put on a backpack and rode my bike to their home in Beverly Hills,' remembered Benny of his arrival at the Elliots. 'I never left.'

Moving into a room converted from an old garage, Benny was soon attending the exclusive Beverly Hills High School, as featured on the TV show *Beverly Hills 90210* – the same school attended by maverick actor Nicolas Cage. Formally adopted by the Elliots, Benny Medina made the most of the new opportunity life had given him, rising through the ranks in the music industry. By the time the 1990's dawned, the 31-year-old had begun to dream of turning his rags-to-riches story into a TV series.

Meanwhile, Will Smith was making connections in Hollywood. Invited backstage during the taping of an *Arsenio Hall Show* tribute to the life and career of black musician, composer and record producer Quincy Jones, he took the opportunity to network with people in the entertainment industry.

Hanging out backstage, Will got chatting to an amiable record executive named Benny Medina. During their conversation, Benny mentioned his idea for a TV show based on a black kid coming from the wrong side of the tracks to live with a rich Beverly Hills family. He was preparing to pitch the idea to the NBC network and felt the Fresh Prince himself might be the ideal talent to play the lead. Will could not believe his luck, but felt it was too early to get excited about a backstage chat during a first meeting. Nevertheless, as he said good-bye to Will in the parking lot outside the TV studio, Benny Medina promised to be in touch.

Medina's next move was to rope Quincy Jones into the project, to gain him credibility in the eyes of sceptical TV executives. Jones was well aware of Will Smith's musical success, and agreed he would be perfect for the part of the inner city kid living with a rich Beverly Hills family. As a final twist to the story, Jones and Medina decided to make the rich family black instead of white like the Elliots. Jones also happened to know that NBC were searching for a half-hour sitcom to fill the 8pm slot on a Monday night, where the cute alien-among-us show *ALF* was drawing to a close. Jones knew NBC needed a family-oriented show as a replacement, and a family-friendly rapper might just make the perfect lead.

The approach to NBC went well, but the whole project nearly collapsed when one simple question was asked of Will Smith – 'Can he act?' NBC's head of entertainment Brandon Tartikoff had watched some videos of Will on *Yo! MTV Raps*, courtesy of Quincy Jones, but was not convinced. Will had never played a real character nor delivered any serious dialogue. The executives loved the idea for the show and were willing to buy it, but were worried that, in Will Smith, they had an inexperienced lead who, if he did not destroy the show straight off, would need too much hand-holding.

But Medina and Jones would not back down. Jones, talking later in *TV Guide*, dubbed Will 'a monster talent', while Medina was convinced the young rapper would have 'real appeal on the screen'. They were prepared to fight for their chosen star, even if they risked losing the show.

Their assurances were not enough. The TV bosses wanted to see Will audition, to be sure he could transfer the talent evident in the music videos to a sitcom format. Medina, however, could not track Will down as he was playing some concerts across the States with Jeff Townes in a concerted effort to pay back the IRS. Medina finally found him in Indiana. Sensing the chance of a lifetime, Will travelled back to California overnight to perform in front of the TV moguls.

'For the first six episodes of *Fresh Prince*, I was so scared that I memorised the entire script.'

The audition took place at Quincy Jones' mansion, where Will was given time to rehearse in one of many bedrooms. 'He picked up this lousy script and read life into lines he had never seen before, in front of the network brass and everyone,' said Medina. 'Afterwards, I realised I had just sat through one of those moments that people always talk about. Once he was in front of the camera, he had the ability to completely capture your attention and really hold onto it.'

Although NBC had been sceptical of Will's acting talents, they realised a popular rap artist would attract a sizeable chunk of the youth audience. The executives wanted more than a quick ratings fix, however – they were hoping for a show with 'legs', that would run for several years and build a strong following. They needed an actor more than a rapper.

Any lurking doubts were dispelled by the show Will put on at the home of Quincy Jones. 'It was clear to me right away that this guy was a natural,' claimed

Despite Will never having acted before, he charmed everyone by his natural abilities as an actor.

NBC executive Warren Littlefield. 'I would go up and down the halls saying, "We have to do something with him." Will read from the script and just nailed it. I sat there thinking, "Whoa! Just bottle this guy."'

Will's performance sealed the deal, and he was ecstatic. Although the show would be produced in a hip-hop style and draw on his rapping smarts, it was a chance to expand his popularity and make a bigger name for himself in the world of mainstream entertainment. Not only that, but the pay cheques from the TV show would go a long way towards resolving his outstanding problems with the IRS. The Fresh Prince was about to make a fresh start.

With *The Fresh Prince of Bel-Air* about to enter production, Will Smith was facing the biggest challenge of his career so far. He was starting from scratch in a new medium with new rules, and would have to prove himself all over again.

'I always knew I had to work at it,' said Will of his prime role in the new sitcom. 'For the first six episodes of *Fresh Prince*, I was so scared that I memorised the entire script. I was sure that, at some point, that they were going to find out that I didn't know how to act, so I just sat down and learned every single stage direction and every piece of dialogue. In the early shows, you can actually see me mouthing everybody else's lines.'

This dedication was the legacy of learning things the hard way. 'Jeff and I, back in Philly, we knew that we had to be practising while the other guys were eating. We had to be practising while the other guys were sleeping. We went to school and practised, and that was it. People who are successful people often think that their success must be because somebody liked them or gave them preferential treatment. The bottom line is, how hard are you willing to work?'

There was no question that Will was willing to work at making a success of *The Fresh Prince*. The show had him playing a combination of himself and Benny Medina, a kid from Philadelphia who moves in with his rich cousins in Bel-Air. 'Will had a straight-ahead African-American background,' noted Medina. 'He was not a ghetto boy, not privileged, but an adequate background. That was just enough to create that self-starter – someone who is ambitious and creative.'

To realise the premise of the show, NBC hired Andy and Susan Borowitz, a married sitcom-writing team who had masterminded the success of the series *Family Ties*, which launched Michael J. Fox into a cinema career. Lacking any knowledge of rap music or of Will Smith himself, a three-week immersion in the world of hip-hop through videos, CDs and endless talk with Will proved to be an education. 'It was a whirlwind thing,' admitted Susan Borowitz.

The Borowitzes created a family of characters for Will to interact with: his uncle, legal eagle Philip Banks, played by James Avery, veteran of many successful drama series; aunt Vivian, whose part was taken by Broadway actress Janet Hubert-Whitten (replaced by Daphne Maxwell Reid in 1993); cousin Hilary, a valley girl, was played by Karyn Parsons; preppy cousin Carlton was Alfonso Ribeiro, another Broadway and TV veteran despite his youth; and cousin Ashley, in the form of twelve-year-old Tatyana M. Ali, an actress since the age of six who had appeared on *The Cosby Show*. It was a formidable line-up, headed by a rapper from Philly who had never acted before.

Because of Will's inexperience, there was still some doubt among the NBC executives whether this hip-hop comedy series would be able to draw a large audience. 'There was kind of a concern about the unknown,' admitted Will as the series debuted at the time of his 22nd birthday in September 1990. 'I was one of the first of the hip-hop generation on television, so there was a sense of wonder if it was going to translate, about how America would accept this hip-hoppin', be-boppin', fast-talking kind of black guy.'

But even Will's self-confidence took a beating after he watched the pilot show, simply entitled *The Fresh Prince Project*. 'There were things I could have done better,' he confessed. 'I missed the rhythm, I didn't quite hit the laughs.'

'Eddie [Murphy] is the only person I ever imitated. He inspired a generation of black comedians, in the same way that Richard Pryor had.'

Consequently, NBC arranged a series of private viewings in front of test audiences, an approach more often used for feature films. They were surprised to discover that the show turned out to be their highest-testing comedy show ever, even beating the scores reached by *The Cosby Show* when it was tested with younger audiences.

Buoyed up by the test results, NBC began to hype the series. As well as meeting with immediate success – coming alternately first or second in the ratings – it also won some rave reviews. *The New York Times* boosted Will's confidence with their acclaim: 'Smith not only can sing, write and dance – he can clearly act, too.' *TV Guide* – the bible of American television – gave the show an immediate boost, claiming 'Will Smith's enjoyment of his role is infectious.'

Enthused with his success, Will was nonetheless wary of the hype that surrounded it. 'Out of my excitement,' admitted NBC entertainment head Tartikoff, 'I made a lot of predictions. Sometimes Will would come up to me and say, "Man, don't compare me with Eddie Murphy. That's putting a lot on my shoulders." I'd tell him, "Will, it's out of love. I was there when Eddie was nineteen, and I saw what he did with his career and talent. Now I see it in you." I feel like I've been a witness at the accident twice.'

Will's initial nerves soon evaporated when The Fresh Prince of Bel-Air'*s success became obvious to all.*

Will was cautious about being too closely compared to Murphy, who had been one of his acting idols when he was growing up. 'Eddie is the only person I ever imitated,' he admitted. 'He inspired a generation of black comedians, in the same way that Richard Pryor had. He's the person that made me see that, okay, maybe I can do this. Because I had never thought about acting, but seeing Eddie, and being able to stand in front of the mirror and deliver Eddie Murphy lines in the way that he delivers them, made me feel that I could do it.'

The comparisons, Will felt, should not be allowed to eclipse his personal ambitions. 'I am nowhere near being Eddie Murphy,' he'd protested in 1990.

'Please, let me get one episode behind me. And give me four or five years!'

For his part, Benny Medina, who had become Will's personal manager, was sure the Fresh Prince had a bright future ahead of him. 'Will is one of those fated people,' he claimed. 'He's one of those destined people, somebody who somehow makes sure he hits the mark he's supposed to . . . He has a likeability factor that I haven't seen in many people in this business. And he is hungry. With those qualities, you don't anticipate any boundaries.'

Will put much of himself into the television character of the Fresh Prince – the ideal approach for a novice actor. 'The character is me,' he admitted in *Interview* magazine. 'I'm not having to do too much acting – I'm just being myself. No-one ever debated that. Everybody understood that I was going to have to deliver that character, because there weren't too many writers in Hollywood that could relate to him.' It was an analysis with which his mother agreed after watching the pilot episode: 'You're not doing anything you didn't do around here,' she told her now-famous son.

Much of Will's life in Philadelphia followed him to the TV show – including his rapping partner Jeff Townes, who played the character of Jazz on and off for most of the six–year run. While Will's new career was sure to interfere with their musical endeavours, the duo quickly agreed to work on a new album during the show's summer break.

'I can't believe how many mistakes I made,' admitted Will, looking back on the early episodes of *Fresh Prince*. 'I can't stand to watch myself. The only thing that saved me on the show was that everybody else in the cast was funny.'

In the early days on the show, Will would miss the marks on the floor which showed him where to stand or would deliver his lines so quietly that the microphone would fail to pick him up. Director Debbie Allen had to encourage Will to just be himself, in the hope of getting a more animated performance from the novice TV actor.

Even young Tatyana Ali thought Will had a lot to learn: 'I couldn't believe how bad an actor he was,' she confided. 'I'd do a scene with him and he'd mouth my words while I was doing my lines . . . if you look at the old shows, you can see it. At first we weren't pals.'

Will was determined to learn as he worked however, picking up tips from his much more experienced co-stars, even twelve-year-old Ali. 'People were expecting a lot,' he recalled of his fear of letting down his co-stars, Quincy Jones and Brandon Tartikoff if he did not improve quickly. 'I have a natural feel, but let me practice first so I can be proud of what I do. This is really new. I had to learn not to look at the camera. In music videos, that's what you do!'

Critics were prepared to see Will Smith fall on his face, questioning writers/producers Andy and Susan Borowitz about their leading man's ability to carry the show. 'We are seeing improvements every day,' they claimed during the taping of the first season. 'Will has natural ability. It's not like we pulled some schmoe off the street.'

Now he had settled his debts with the IRS, Will considered employing an acting coach – despite the fact that Quincy Jones, whose company was producing the show, insisted he did not need lessons. The Fresh Prince himself, however, found that being touted as the next Eddie Murphy made people like James Avery reluctant to offer him advice. 'After that first year,' recalled Avery, 'Will said to us, "I'm really mad at you people. You let me get out there on stage and make a fool of myself."'

Envy also played a part in the on-set tensions during the first year. Most of the cast had been acting for many years, and were none too happy at being outshone by a 21-year-old upstart rapper who fluffed his lines and stumbled about in front of the camera.

One of Will's most helpful mentors was Bill Cosby, who broke the mould for black actors on TV by co-starring in the sixties espionage show *I Spy,* before graduating to movies and *The Cosby Show.* Will had complained to Cosby about problems he was having with the *Fresh Prince* scripts. Cosby said he should go home and write his own, if he thought it was so easy. Taking Cosby at his word, Will discovered it was a lot harder than he had thought. 'When I met the writers the next day, I had a lot less anger and a lot more understanding of the process.'

From rap star to prime-time TV star was a big change, but bigger changes overtook Will in his private life. He had gone from *nouveau riche* kid to indebted bankrupt, and now, thanks to *The Fresh Prince of Bel-Air,* was swinging back again. His debts paid off, he was determined to take a different approach to this second chance at fame and fortune at the age of 22.

'I've already enjoyed success, and it didn't change me,' claimed Will prior to the pilot show's screening. 'I'm ready. Success has already gone to my head – I've already been selfish and didn't listen to advice.'

This time he would listen to advice: to his family, and to the professional, financial and career advisers he could now afford to employ. With Benny Medina as his personal manager, Will also had a personal friend and colleague guiding his career and looking out for his best interests.

Will's home in Los Angeles – a small flat in Burbank near to the NBC studio where his TV show was taped – was markedly different to the Philadelphia mansion he once owned. Cramped though it was, he still filled out the interior much as he had done back in Philly, with a mini-pool table dominating the living room, a top-of-the-range stereo system and numerous video games. Though it was a comfortable life, Will was certainly not 'livin' large'.

At the age of 22, Will was a different man to the Philadelphia teenager he had once been. Spurning parties, he claimed, 'I'm an in-the-house type of person. I'm not out at clubs or anything like that. I don't hang out with too many new people. I don't need a social life. I've got to work now, I'll get a social life when I'm 30. I'm not into the LA lifestyle anyway. It takes your mind off work.'

In fact, he no longer even needed to get out and meet girls – having already met and fallen in love with an aspiring model. Tanya Moore was a nineteen-year-old student at San Diego State University when Will met her at a 1988 Jazzy Jeff and the Fresh Prince gig on campus. According to Moore, 'Will just came right up to me and said I was the girl of his dreams.'

'Going into the movies, I wanted to do something a little different and then maybe down the line get back into the comedies.'

The pair began dating and stayed in touch throughout Will's move from Philadelphia to Los Angeles as he switched from rapper to sitcom star. Of the entourage who helped Will spend his money during his first flush of fame, Tanya was one of the few who stuck with the fallen star during the low period that ensued. As Will prepared for *The Fresh Prince*, Moore stayed loyally by his side. 'We just hang out,' he claimed. 'What's good about Tanya is she thinks like a guy, so I don't miss my buddies. It's like, I can't relate to somebody crying because she broke a fingernail.'

Although the relationship was to last three years, it seems to have been a puppy love romance that allowed Will to grow emotionally as he went through his financial troubles and learned to cope with fame anew. Despite Moore's support during his TV debut, their time together quickly drew to a close. 'Will is real cool about everything,' she said of his second chance at fame. 'He's like none of this has hit him.'

During 1991 Will worked with Jeff Townes on *Homebase*, their fourth album together. Although the TV show was taking off, he was still determined to keep his career options open. Despite plans to record during the hiatus in production on

Fresh Prince, however a scheduling clash meant the two demands on Will's time overlapped. 'I'm doing the show from nine to five, and from six to midnight I'm in the studio working on the album. But as long as I get my eight hours of sleep, I'm fine.' It was this workload, as much as his own attitude to LA society, that explained Will's lack of a social life during most of 1991.

Things were working out for Will Smith – from being on the brink of bankruptcy to prime-time TV stardom was a huge turnaround and he was enjoying the fame and sharing the limelight with his girlfriend, Tanya Moore. As he prepared to return from a second series of *The Fresh Prince of Bel-Air* in 1991-92, Will also found his acting ambitions turning toward the big screen.

'I studied the careers of people who had made successful transitions from television to film: Tom Hanks, Eddie Murphy, Jim Carrey.'

With his acting ability improving in leaps and bounds, Will decided he needed the practical experience of shooting a couple of films. The easy route would have been to bring the equivalent of *Fresh Prince* to the big screen, but he had deliberately avoided that when he turned down *House Party* two years before. 'People can see me do that [comedy] on the show,' he explained. 'Going into the movies, I wanted to do something a little different and then maybe down the line get back into the comedies. Robin Williams and Tom Hanks go back and forth, but I think from watching their careers it's really important to make it clear that you can do something other than comedies.'

Watching other actors closely became central to Will's plan. 'I studied the careers of people who had made successful transitions from television to film: Tom Hanks, Eddie Murphy, Jim Carrey. I basically went in and broke it down – why were these people successful? It came down to a couple of basic elements. They were "regular guys". You looked at them and you felt you had a great sense of who this person was when they were at home with their wife and kids. Just a regular guy. I thought, Well, hell, why can't the next regular guy be me?'

Experience had taught Will not to jump at the first film offer that came his way. Approached very early in the run of *Fresh Prince* to take the leading role in a low-budget science fiction film, though he was a fan of the genre he claimed he was not ready for a big screen role just yet. By the time Will felt able to turn his attention to movies he had decided to start small, taking a role in an ensemble movie very different from his real life and his small-screen life on *Fresh Prince*.

Smith was relieved to be working with such experienced actors as Whoopi Goldberg and Ted Danson in Made in America.

A modest independent film, *Where the Day Takes You* (1992) was about the lives of a group of homeless street kids in Los Angeles. Directed by Marc Rocco, it featured Dermot Mulroney telling his story to an off-screen prison psychologist (voiced by *Sex, Lies and Videotape* star Laura San Giacomo). It also starred Sean Astin, Balthazar Getty, James Le Gross, *Twin Peaks'* Lara Flynn Boyle, Ricki Lake, Adam Baldwin, David Arquette and Will Smith – who played a wheelchair-bound paraplegic, billed tenth in the credits.

The character of Manny was as far from Will's *Fresh Prince* image as possible. Making the most of his two brief scenes, including one in which he is beaten up and tipped out of his wheelchair by a street thug, the future big-screen star was performing with casting directors very much in mind.

Will was also impressed by the message of the film. 'Just seeing how people ignore the homeless was an amazing lesson,' he observed of his in-character experience. 'I was in full make-up on Hollywood Boulevard, and people didn't know me. It was a revelation seeing how cold people could be.'

Smith would concrete his reputation as an actor in Made in America, *seen here with actress Nia Long.*

Although not widely seen – the film enjoyed a brief cinema release in the US in September 1992 before going to video and cable TV – Will's low-key performance brought him to the attention of casting directors who previously only knew him for *The Fresh Prince*. He started to receive a variety of scripts, mostly low-budget rip-offs of the latest box-office hit.

It was soon announced in the Hollywood trade press that Will would be taking the lead role in science-fiction creature-feature *Biofeed,* and would follow it up with the lead in a baseball movie entitled *Scout.* Neither film was made, but it was a sign of Will's growing popularity that his name was used in a mischevious attempt to kick-start production.

Will's second cinema film enjoyed a wider distribution but only a lukewarm critical reception. In *Made in America* (1993), Whoopi Goldberg played a single mother whose daughter sets out to discover her biological father, only to find he was white sperm donor Ted Danson (*Cheers*). Actress Nia Long played the daughter, while Will was cast in a small role as her boyfriend. Nia would go on to play Will's girlfriend in later episodes of *The Fresh Prince of Bel-Air* – a role that Will's second wife, actress Jada Pinkett, had also auditioned for but failed to win on account of being 'too short'.

Will was relieved that it was someone as experienced as Whoopi Goldberg, rather than himself, who was carrying the movie. 'Working with Whoopi was really cool,' he said of her. 'I learned a lot, including how to behave between scenes.' On the set of *The Fresh Prince of Bel-Air*, he had become known as a practical joker, tolerated on account of being the star of the show. He was quick to discover such antics would not endear him to the cast and crew on an expensive film set.

Will's growing celebrity followed him to a location shoot in San Francisco for *Made in America,* where he found himself mobbed by fans of his music and his TV show. Posing for photos and happy to sign autographs, Will's following was noticed by a couple of film producers visiting the shoot, Arnon Milchan and Michael Douglas. 'There were, I guess, about twenty girls across the street,' remembered Will. 'I walked out and the girls started screaming. Arnon and Michael Douglas were, like, "What the hell are they screaming about?" Then they saw it was for me and said, "Oh, yeah, we definitely have to do some business with this guy."'

None of this went to Will's head. He was still determined to learn all he could about the industry and develop his acting abilities, but came to consider *Made in America* a mis-step in his attempt to distance himself from *The Fresh Prince of Bel-Air.* 'Allowing the *Fresh Prince* character to follow me into the film was a mistake,' he said of the boyfriend role. 'I broke my rule and that won't happen again.'

It was, however, his role in *Made in America* which would lead to his landing the plum role of Paul, the con man in the critically acclaimed film version of the Broadway hit *Six Degrees of Separation* – a film that would put Will Smith firmly on the road to Hollywood stardom.

04

SHADOW DREAMS

Up until the end of his relationship with aspiring model Tanya Moore, Will Smith's romantic life had been fairly quiet. While he was consistently unwilling to discuss their break-up, there's little doubt that Will's relentless work schedule had a large role to play. When rumours that Tanya had struck up a relationship with Johnny Gill of the band New Edition began to circulate, it was the last straw. Will would fall into his next relationship on the rebound from Tanya Moore.

He put the collapse of his first major romance down to 'the green eyed monster', jealousy – but on her part not his, suggesting Tanya could not cope with the kind of attention the Fresh Prince was now attracting. 'When I got famous, women started looking at me differently,' he claimed. 'The girl I was with, no matter how much we were in love, just couldn't accept the fact that other women were looking at me and screaming at me on stage. And love just couldn't beat life, not in my situation.'

Will Smith with his first wife Sheree Zampino. The relationship would
soon flounder, due to Smith's increasingly intense work schedule.

While visiting an actor friend on the set of the sitcom *A Different World* in 1991, Will met Sheree Zampino, a fashion design student. For months, Will would pursue her over the telephone while Sheree resisted the advances of the famous Fresh Prince. 'She defuses the negative aspects of my personality,' said Will of Sheree. 'There was always a yearning in me to do the right thing and be a good person. It took me two years of my vast wellspring of charm to get Sheree to marry me.' Once Sheree had agreed to go out with Will, he spent the remainder of that year seriously seducing her, capping it with a proposal of marriage as the year drew to a close. He was determined not to let this one get away, at any cost.

'I've always been a one-girl guy. I was never a playboy. I don't know why, but I just really prefer to be with one person.'

'It was Christmas Eve,' recalled Will. 'Sheree was in Los Angeles and she thought I was flying to Philadelphia to spend Christmas with my family. What I actually did was go to the airport to meet my brother, Harry. He had flown in to bring me the ring I'd bought from a friend of mine in Philadelphia. Then I went home and called Sheree and told her that I had forgotten some important papers. Could she please go to my house and grab them for me? I really needed these papers. So, she drove there and when she got inside, I was waiting for her in the bedroom on one knee with the ring, and I proposed to her there.'

It was a short step from here to the star-studded marriage ceremony on 9 May 1992. The wedding took place at the exclusive Four Seasons Biltmore Hotel in Santa Barbara and cost the couple over $50,000 – a sum Will could easily afford, now that his IRS troubles were settled and his TV show was topping the ratings. The couple – both aged 23 at the time – said their marriage vows in the open air overlooking the Pacific ocean. Among the 125 friends and family members in attendance were Will's brother Harry, as the ring bearer and best man, and Jazzy Jeff, as ever at his rapping partner's side. Among the celebrities in attendance were actor Denzel Washington and basketball star Magic Johnson.

For a while Will and Sheree were trumpeted by *Ebony* magazine as one of America's 'ten hottest couples'. They were constantly together, even to the extent of Sheree sitting in on press interviews to promote *The Fresh Prince*. The pair quickly worked up a repartee which involved mock sparring and attempted one-upmanship. As Will put it, 'Sheree and I have got this comedy battle going.'

Occasionally, however, the pretend arguments would spill over into real ones, while – as with Tanya – Will's heavy work schedule also began to take its toll. However, the couple decided to put aside their difficulties when Sheree announced she was pregnant.

'This is the most exciting thing,' Will declared enthusiastically to the press. 'Our baby is going to be a real life prince or princess of Bel-Air.' Young 'prince' Willard C. Smith III was born in December 1992. Although faithfully continuing the Smith family naming tradition, Will did not want his son to be another 'Will junior' – instead, he and Sheree decided to call him by the nickname 'Trey' (a punning corruption of 'Three', as in Will Smith the third).

The responsibility of fatherhood soon dawned on Will. 'I realised things were different now. Suddenly, I felt this huge yoke of responsibility. Being a dad changes everything. Things had to be different now, starting on the car ride home from the hospital. I made a vow to stay healthy and eat right, as it's not just for me any more.' Soon after the doctor handed him his first born child, Will's new safety regime imposed slower speeds and more care at junctions on the drive home. 'The doctor handed him to me, but I also felt God metaphysically handed him to me', he said of the most momentous event of his life so far. The birth of his son, and the feelings he experienced, would inspire Will's song 'Just the Two of Us', in which he directly addresses Trey.

Despite their difficulties and Will's professional commitments, he was determined he and Sheree would stay together, especially for the sake of Trey. 'I've always been a one-girl guy,' said Will. 'I was never a playboy. I don't know why, but I just really prefer to be with one person.'

The casting of Will Smith – regarded in 1993 as strictly a rap singer and sitcom star – in the film version of John Guare's Tony Award-winning play *Six Degrees of Separation* was described by the *Los Angeles Times* as 'the most audacious example of Hollywood casting against type since Donna Reed played a hooker in *From Here to Eternity*'.

Will was preparing to star alongside long-established actors Stockard Channing and Donald Sutherland as Paul, a gay con artist who charms his way into the home of Manhattan socialites by pretending to be the son of black actor Sidney Poitier. 'I met him,' said Will of the star of sign-of-the-times 1960's features like *Guess Who's Coming to Dinner* (1967) and *In the Heat of the Night* (1967). 'He kind of looked at me and said, "Well, you're almost handsome enough to be my son!"'

It was important to Will that his first major film role should be so very different from his character in *The Fresh Prince of Bel-Air*, which by this time was now a significant domestic ratings hit. 'If you lined up a hundred films, this one would be the last one people would expect me to do,' he admitted. '*Six Degrees* was the scariest choice that I've ever had to make in my career.'

Having examined the careers of other actors who made a successful move from television to movies, Will knew that it was an enterprise fraught with difficulties. 'In general television actors don't really get respect in the world of film,' he acknowledged, relating it to his own experience. 'On *The Fresh Prince of Bel-Air* I never really had an opportunity to show anything beyond telling jokes and having fun and being silly. So there was no reason for anyone to believe that there was any depth beyond that. Just to get *Six Degrees* and to be able to work as hard as I worked was just a really great opportunity for me to prove a couple of people wrong.'

'Showing you can do a complete 180 degree turn is what makes the movie industry sit up and pay attention.'

John Guare's play was based on a real life incident which took place in New York in the mid-eighties. A black nineteen year-old con artist managed to pull off the same trick twice, fooling two prominent wealthy families into allowing him into their circle. Claiming to be Paul Poitier, son of Sidney Poitier, the conman blamed his dishevelled appearance on having been mugged, when he turned up on the doorstep of the target family whose background he had exhaustedly researched. Shelter, friendship and even financial donations would follow.

Both the play and the film adaptation tackle the deceptive nature of surface appearances, plus the issues of racism and homophobia. Taking this role would be a dramatic challenge for any actor, but it was a particular gamble with Will's career.

It was for these very reasons that Will Smith set out to win the role. 'Showing you can do a complete 180 degree turn is what makes the movie industry sit up and pay attention,' he explained. 'If I don't do a good job, it's a risk. The plan was always to minimise the downside. It was so different from anything I'd ever done before, that even if I failed, I didn't think it could hurt me. In some ways, it was so risky that it was completely safe.'

Will Smith gambled his entire acting career on playing the leading role in Six Degrees of Separation, *a gamble that would pay off. He co-starred with Donald Sutherland and Stockard Channing.*

Determined to escape the Fresh Prince, Will wanted to connect for the first time with a distinctly adult audience. 'This isn't a movie you'll take your kids to,' said Will. 'The biggest consideration for me was that if I pulled this role off, then I'd be a legitimate actor. Film is the medium to succeed in. I want to be able to be accepted in any type of endeavour I choose.'

Smith with fellow actors Heather Graham and Eric Thal in Six Degrees of Separation.

Actress Stockard Channing, who originated the role of matriarch Ouisa Kittredge on stage in New York and London, was already attached to the film under conditions set by author John Guare when selling the rights to MGM. Veteran actor Donald Sutherland had been cast as her art dealer husband, the curiously named Flan Kittredge. When Guare visited the set of *The Fresh Prince of Bel-Air* to meet Will Smith, he was aware the young actor had launched a personal media campaign to win the part of Paul.

Will had prepared a 'pitch', a presentation for Guare which included all the positive reasons for casting him in the film. However as soon as Guare met Will he felt he had found Paul. 'I met him with trepidation,' recalled the playwright, 'but within five minutes, I was impressed. Except for his charm, the Will I meet was not the Fresh Prince. That's one eighth of what he can do.'

That meeting was enough for Guare to recommend the actor to director Fred Schepisi. Aware of Will's rap and sitcom background, the director was not so quickly convinced. 'Everybody got excited about Will,' Schepisi remembered, 'but I was a little more cautious. I interviewed a lot of actors. Will tried to convince me that he'd do whatever it would take, would go through whatever process, was sure he could get himself prepared.'

Producer Arnon Milchan (who was behind *Made in America*) was on Will's side too, but Schepisi remained to be convinced. In an effort to clinch the part, Will turned up to a meeting with the director in a three-piece suit with his charm turned up to the maximum, every bit as persuasive as the conman in the play. As Schepisi said: 'He did a number on me, with such incredible confidence and charm that his very act of trying to convince me of his abilities did exactly that. He was worth taking a chance on.'

Will's main competition for the part had been Courtney B. Vance, who won rave reviews in the role in the New York production. By the time of casting the film, Vance was considered too old for the part of the college-age conman. That left Schepisi looking at 'all sorts of hot, young actors' before deciding to go with Will. For Will himself the process had been agonising, having been acutely aware he was not the first choice. 'Actually, they didn't want me for the role,' he admitted. 'But Arnon Milchan, the guy who was [partially] financing it, basically said, "If you don't use Will Smith, you don't have a movie."'

Confirmed in the role, with the complete script in front of him to begin his preparation, Will was struck by two realisations: 'My first impression was that this was going to be the most difficult thing I ever had to do in entertainment,' he explained, before succinctly summing up his second impression as: 'Oh shit, he's homosexual!'

Will was suddenly aware of the potential for a homophobic backlash against him, his music and even the TV show. 'My big concern was for my rap career – you don't see too many rappers playing homosexual roles in films. The origins of the music are about masculinity, how tough you can be. So I was concerned about how my credibility would be affected.'

So worried was Will about this aspect of the role that he approached Denzel Washington – then the most successful black actor in Hollywood and a guest at Will's wedding to Sheree – for advice. 'I wanted to get his opinion on how people look at the roles you choose,' explained Will. 'Denzel said white people generally look at a movie as acting. They accept the actors for who they are, and the role is separate. But black people, because they have so few heroes in film, tend to hold the artists personally responsible for the roles they choose.'

As far as Washington was concerned the part of Paul was a good move, but he also warned him: 'You can act all you want, but don't do any physical scenes.' According to Will, Washington told him simply, 'Don't be kissing no man!'

The script initially featured a kiss between Will's character and his source of information on the Kittredges, actor Anthony Michael Hall. During shooting, director Fred Schepisi shot Will from behind during the lip-locking scene, having decided the film did not need any explicit homo-eroticism to make it work. This approach unknowingly avoided a looming conflict, as Will had not revealed his reluctance to tackle the kissing scene. 'I waited till they gave me my cheque to tell them that I wasn't going to do what the script called for,' he later admitted. 'Black fans can't afford to see us in compromising roles. All of that other stuff is acting, but if I kissed him, I kissed him for real.'

It was an attitude Will was to revise in later years, explaining, in an interview

'I learned a valuable lesson in that you do the audience a disservice if you don't completely commit to the character. If you are not going to commit, then don't take it.'

for *Ebony*, that 'I learned a valuable lesson in that you do the audience a disservice if you don't completely commit to the character. If you are not going to commit, then don't take it. It was very immature on my part . . . I was thinking, "What are my friends in Philly going to think about this?" I wasn't emotionally stable enough to artistically commit to that aspect of the film.'

Will later admitted that his reservations about the character's sexuality had led to accusations of homophobia. 'I think I've almost been forgiven now,' he said years later. 'That was just a difficult time for me. If I had to do it over again, I would do it differently. I don't know if I would kiss a man, but I know that I would do it or I wouldn't do the film at all.'

In preparation for the role, Will went to see productions of the play in three cities – New York, Los Angeles and London – to gain a variety of perspectives on the lead role. This unprecedented acting challenge would mean changing his accent and manner of speaking, leading him to engage the services of a dialogue coach for eighteen weeks. The process of changing his identity for the role reflected the similar tactics used by his character to fool the Kittredge clan. 'This character had to learn to walk and talk and act,' noted Will of conman Paul. 'And I had to learn to walk and talk and act to play him.' Will was also determined to get into shape for the role, employing a personal fitness trainer to beef up his skinny physique.

Will went through a metamorphic change to play the leading role in Six Degrees of Separation.

For the first time, in *Six Degrees of Separation* he would play a character far removed from himself – on *The Fresh Prince of Bel-Air* he was simply Will Smith writ large, while both *Where the Day Takes You* and *Made in America* had been variations on his own personality. 'It was the first time I ever had to be someone else. All of your instincts and all of the things that you've worked on, all the faces you learn to make and all of your tools are stripped. And you're fighting a battle, but you can't use any of the weapons that you've used your whole life, so you have to start from scratch . . . It was a whole new arena with nothing that I've worked with before, not even my own voice . . . the role was so different from me that

I had to adjust every aspect of myself to play it.'

Will also hoped the role would allow him to be taken seriously by directors he dreamed of working with. 'I wanted to work with Spike Lee and John Singleton,' he remembered. 'They were both kind of like, "Oh, he's this TV guy. We've never really seen him do anything." I needed to do a film like *Six Degrees* in order for these people to consider me. Spike Lee would never consider me for a role, because *The Fresh Prince of Bel-Air* is all he's ever seen. How would he know that I could do what he demands of an actor?'

For director Schepisi, Will's painstaking preparation was paramount to the success of the role. 'Will had a reputation and a name, but this was a work of more substance,' said the director, 'we weren't expecting to teach him about the whole acting experience, but we wanted him to have a healthy respect for what's involved.'

As well as the advice of Denzel Washington, Will had co-stars Stockard Channing and Donald Sutherland to draw on for help in bringing his character to life. 'Stockard Channing was really great because she was a walking encyclopaedia of *Six Degrees*,' said Will of the Tony Award-winning actress. 'She had done it with so many different people, so many different times, that if I was feeling a little uncomfortable about something, she knew five or six ways that other people had tried it. All of the problems that I may have had, she had already discussed with people previously. So she was very clear about what she wanted to do, and she was very open about things that she had experienced with it.'

It was on the advice of Channing that Will decided not to memorise a thirty-page scene revolving around a telephone conversation, including a lot of dialogue spoken by his character. 'It almost made me not want to take the role,' he admitted of the fear of forgetting his lines. Channing, however, suggested that he should play to his strengths. Although *The Fresh Prince of Bel-Air* depended on delivery of punchlines and gags, there had been room for improvisation and personal quirks. Channing wanted to play up the emotional content of the telephone conversation scene, rather than adhering to the specific words on the page. It was an approach that opened up a whole new world to Will, bringing him to grips with the material, crafting a performance of great depth and maturity for such a young and inexperienced actor.

For her part, Channing believed the role indicated a solid future for Will as a film actor. 'If he had registered any angst or insecurity, he wouldn't have gotten the role,' she opined, stressing that for all the acting experience of Sutherland and herself, neither of them outshone Will. 'I don't think there's any discrepancy. I don't feel it at all. There's probably a bigger gap between Donald and myself than between me and Will in sheer film experience.'

The producer of *Six Degrees of Separation*, Ric Kidney, felt that Will's natural

'I always had that square-looking
hairdo, and I liked it, even though
it made my ears stick out.
One guy once told me that I looked
like a car with the doors open.'

'From the beginning, this movie [MIB] is just fun. It can be really silly and it can be really smart. This is the type of movie that will mark points in people's lives.'

'With all that jumping and shooting when you're making an action movie, it brings out all that testosterone. Everybody has an action hero in them; everyone wants to kick in a door and shoot somebody.'

talents and charm outweighed his lack of acting experience. 'Paul has to captivate you,' he said of the film's central character. 'The night he comes to the house and meets these people, he captivates them and the audience.'

Will's performance captivated film audiences and critics alike, when the modestly-budgeted (fifteen million dollar) production was released in 1993. *Entertainment Weekly* were impressed by his dramatic debut: 'Will Smith, in an impressive performance, makes Paul easy to watch – as smooth and transparent as glass.' For *People* magazine, the performance was nothing short of 'remarkable', while *Time* noted that 'as Paul, Will Smith is needy, daring, insinuating'. For the

'I hope I did a good job on *Six Degrees*. It was the best film experience I could have had. It encouraged me to do more.'

Hollywood Reporter, Will was 'charismatically winning as the mystery kid'.

The reviews were unanimous. The *L.A. Times* claimed that 'the inescapable star, the real winner of *Six Degrees*, is unexpectedly Will Smith, who most of us thought was just a celebrity TV actor rapper flash-in-the-pan. He turns out to be an accomplished, intelligent, moving actor.' *Newsweek* made a very accurate prediction: 'Smith, the rapper and star of TV's *The Fresh Prince of Bel-Air*, is an eye-opener in a complex, tricky part. Will Smith is going to be very big.'

'I hope I did a good job on *Six Degrees*,' reflected Will. 'It was the best film experience I could have had. It encouraged me to do more. My drive was the fact that they didn't want me, they didn't think that I could do it. They thought I was the worst choice you could have for the role. But that gave me the strength and energy to do this. I'm definitely looking for other things. I want to be considered for the blockbuster comedy, but I also want to be considered for the dramatic, artistic pieces. I'll do anything.'

To this day, many people close to Will Smith believe that, in *Six Degrees of Separation,* he had given his best performance – including his mother, father, brother and *Fresh Prince* co-star James Avery, who saw Will's later blockbuster movies as lesser productions: 'He has a lot more talent than these films [*Bad Boys, Independence Day*] show. I think there's a lot more going on there than anyone knows. I think there's a lot more going on there than he is really aware of.'

05
CAUGHT IN THE MIDDLE OF LOVE AND LIFE

For the fourth season of *The Fresh Prince of Bel-Air*, Will Smith had to unlearn everything he had picked up for the part of Paul in *Six Degrees of Separation* and return to his comedy home-boy rapper role of the past three years. It was not an easy task.

'It took six shows to get back up to speed,' he admitted of his struggle to recapture the character. 'I had to watch all the old episodes and go back to my old neighbourhood in Philadelphia and hang with my buddies to get back into the mindset.'

Having put so much work into destroying his Fresh Prince persona for *Six Degrees of Separation*, it was disorientating to return to playing the same limited character. 'I grew tremendously as an actor,' reflected Will. 'At the same time I didn't realise how far you could get lost in a character and I got so far into Paul that when I came back for the fourth season, I was lost. I didn't know what I was

Will Smith as Mike Lowrey in Bad Boys, *becoming a true action-hero in the process.*

doing. I didn't know who my character was. I didn't know how to talk or how to stand. I lost the character of the Fresh Prince.'

Still learning his craft, Will never thought of himself as a method actor who would become immersed so deeply in his character that he lost himself. It came as a shock to find that this was exactly what had happened.

'I was crazy during that movie. Crazy,' Will admitted much later. 'And I didn't realise it. People would say, "What's up with you? Why are you talking like that?" It's probably one of the reasons my first marriage didn't work, but it was an important time. I matured from that experience, almost like coming back from a war. And people noticed. I wasn't the Fresh Prince any more. I'd grown up.'

'The fact that I couldn't act was what made *Fresh Prince* popular.'

Clearly, returning to *The Fresh Prince of Bel-Air* was not going to be easy. In fact, Will feared that having learned more about his craft might actually be a liability on the small screen. 'The fact that I couldn't act was what made *Fresh Prince* popular,' he admitted. 'It was so real. When I started the show, I was pretty much just playing myself, but now my life experience has gone beyond the life experience of the character.'

It was also a culture shock to return to TV production after the leisurely pace of making a feature film. 'You've got five days, period,' he described the tight schedule for each episode. 'You get into the habit of doing things, creating things, quickly. When you get into a movie, the tempo is much slower. It's much easier to find that great line, or that great delivery. You get more time, and there's a lot more space to achieve that perfection.'

The main compensation was that, after each one-week rehearsal period, Will Smith was back to recording every episode in front of a live audience. 'You get the immediate feedback of a live audience in television, which is really great – you know instantly whether it's right or wrong,' he noted. 'The difference with films is you have more of an opportunity to get it right.'

Having gained greater experience in both his professional and personal life, Will was also interested in wielding power behind the scenes of the show. Having dealt with serious issues like inequality and racism in *Six Degrees of Separation*, Will wanted *Fresh Prince* to deal with the realities of life for his character – rather than that of the rich Banks family.

'We're talking about a seventeen-year-old black man from the inner city and there are certain things he should be concerned with – sex and drugs, for two,' noted Will. 'He should have more involvement with friends from the inner city. There should be lots of touchy issues on the show, like prejudice. I want everyone to be enlightened when they watch our show.'

Coupled to this was a desire to sharpen up the humour and make it more topical and relevant to real life. 'I sense a great responsibility to make the show cutting edge, and I will no longer tolerate those things I disagree with,' Will announced, outlining his vision and his avowed intent to control the production. 'I really hate dumb jokes. I'm always fighting it. I keep saying, "Why can't we be more like *Roseanne*?" That's the best show on TV. I'd love our jokes to have meaning beyond the superficial humour.'

However, Will's ambitions for the series and attempts to wield his star power were about to backfire. Tensions had been growing over the years between the cast members, and the producers were aware that Will's more experienced co-stars were reluctant to allow the star to throw his weight around after just one (albeit critically acclaimed) movie. 'In Hollywood there's a great resistance to change,' Will admitted when his efforts were rebuffed behind-the-scenes. 'I'm being met with much opposition.'

The rest of the cast, the producers, writers, and even the network were desperate to maintain the status quo on *The Fresh Prince of Bel-Air*. It was succeeding in its time slot and drawing a large, regular audience – not a formula anyone wanted to tamper with, even at the risk of upsetting the Prince himself.

The question of whether *The Fresh Prince* was peddling a 'soft' version of the 'black experience', as critics had claimed, was becoming an issue behind the scenes. Production/writing team Andy and Susan Borowitz were not about to surrender creative control to Will Smith, even though the criticism that they knew nothing of black urban life was beginning to stick.

The dispute between Will and the producers was mediated by his personal manager, Benny Medina, the man who originated the show in the first place. He agreed with Will that the show had to include more character development, even at the expense of some of the humour. As a result, Will enjoyed more creative input before the scripts were drafted, allowing him to strongly affect their direction. That outcome did not please the Borowitzes, who promptly quit. As Medina put it: 'They decided they'd rather not continue as producers – which none of us was upset about.'

Medina moved quickly to repair the damage, hiring black American TV professional Winifred Hervey-Stallworth as the show's new producer. The change in tone and pace went down well with the cast – and even better with viewers. As Will's input behind the scenes increased, so the show's ratings and the atmosphere on set improved, past tensions dissolving as the actors came to realise they were all doing their best work to date.

The renewed vigour behind *The Fresh Prince of Bel-Air* did not leave the fourth series entirely problem free. Some cast members felt Will Smith was wielding just a little too much power on the set.

Actress Janet Hubert-Whitten, who played Aunt Viv, was suddenly fired. She claimed that Will was behind her departure from the ratings hit. 'Anyone who stands up to Mr Smith on *Fresh Prince* is gone,' she claimed when the story hit the press. 'Yes, I reprimanded him constantly for being rude to people and locking himself in his room, but I did not slander him in any way.'

'Children learn by example and I'm trying to set a good example. I want to be the world's greatest dad in the eyes of my son.'

As far as Will was concerned, Hubert-Whitten's departure was a case of professional jealousy. 'I can say straight up that Janet wanted the show to be *The Aunt Viv of Bel-Air show*,' he claimed in response. 'She's been mad at me all along. She said once: "I've been in this business for ten years and this snotty-nosed punk comes along and gets a show?" No matter what, to her I'm just the anti-Christ.'

Now credited as an executive producer, Will collaborated with Winifred Hervey-Stallworth in auditioning for a replacement actress. They finally settled on Daphne Maxwell Reid, an experienced TV actress who took on the part of Aunt Viv following the character's pregnancy – a storyline that had been developed when the previous Aunt Viv, Hubert-Whitten, really did become pregnant. It was down to Jeff Townes as Jazz, now a regular on the show, to make the only on-screen acknowledgement of the change of actress when he noted: 'You sure have changed since you had that baby.'

Whatever the backstage problems, the cast and crew of *The Fresh Prince of Bel-Air* were at the peak of their collective power during its fourth year on air. Meanwhile, his newfound power in the movie industry raised the question of how long Will Smith could continue as the Fresh Prince.

With his professional life undergoing rapid change, Will's private life was heading the same way. For a while, in public he and Sheree Zampino seemed like a perfect match. Their son Trey often accompanied Will onto the set of *The Fresh Prince*, where he would become the centre of attraction for the cast and crew. Will was keen for his son to see his father at work and equally as keen to reinforce the discipline with which he himself had been raised. 'As Trey grows up, I hope he'll be proud of my work ethic and how I treat people,' said Will, despite the Hubert-Whitten crisis. 'I always try to be nice, try to be positive. Children learn by example and I'm trying to set a good example. I want to be the world's greatest dad in the eyes of my son.'

The youngster was becoming so used to backstage life that he quickly got to know how things worked around a television studio, telling everyone to be quiet when the red recording signal was switched on. The cast and crew doted on Trey, who in turn was respectful to them and always asked permission when he wanted to play with something.

At home, things were not so happy. The production of *Six Degrees of Separation* had taken its toll, with Will away from the family home only shortly after his wedding and the birth of his son. Despite his wish to be the perfect father and husband, such good intentions slipped as he pursued his professional ambitions in the movie industry.

Getting into the character of Paul had become such an all-consuming obsession that it affected Will's new life with Sheree and Trey. 'I didn't know that when you work on a role that hard that it gets inside of you,' he described the onset of their relationship's breakdown. 'When I was doing the character, I became him for a little while. I would block out 72 hours and try and shop like he would shop – just be him. Sheree and I were newlyweds, and I was basically crazy.'

Having demanded – and been granted – more power over the production of *The Fresh Prince of Bel-Air*, it was no longer enough for Will to simply show up and record the show. He was involved in the creation of plotlines, approval of scripts and hiring of guest stars. 'We had a new son,' he recalled of that period. 'My career was taking off. There was lots of pressure that didn't allow the marriage to blossom.'

Determined also to capitalise on his good notices for *Six Degrees of Separation* and expand his feature film opportunities, Sheree and Trey took a backseat to Will's career. It was a situation that could not go on for ever.

Will was desperate to play the part of Robin to Val Kilmer's Batman in Joel Schumacher's *Batman Forever*. As with *Six Degrees of Separation*, he set about lobbying hard for the role, feeling strongly that a black Robin would be a welcome addition to the Batman mythos. This time, however, his tactics failed – after considering rising star Matt Damon, Schumacher awarded the much coveted role to Chris O'Donnell. Despite the disappointment, the ideal racial crossover role was about to come Will's way.

Flamboyant action-film producers Don Simpson and Jerry Bruckheimer had been struggling to bring the comedy-drama buddy-cop thriller *Bad Boys* to the screen. It had started life as a simple idea by Don Simpson, outlined as 'two cops who are brothers and the girl who comes between them'. It was one of many projects the pair had in development as part of their 'visionary alliance' deal at Paramount Pictures, which gave the producers of *Flashdance, Beverly Hills Cop, Top Gun* and *Days of Thunder* carte blanche to produce whatever they liked.

In the early stages of development, *Bad Boys* was planned as a comedy vehicle for *Saturday Night Live* alumni Jon Lovitz and Dana Carvey. Disputes over their salary requirements, however, delayed the scheduled 1993 production. Don Simpson – who had a reputation for 'livin' large', as Will Smith himself might have put it – attempted to seal the deal by inviting Lovitz and Carvey for a weekend in Las Vegas. So freaked was Carvey by the producer's dominant personality, according to Hollywood sources, that he decided not to make the movie, even if they met his two million-dollar salary demand.

This killed the 1993 incarnation of *Bad Boys* before the script was even finished. According to screenwriter James Toback, Simpson had a contingency plan to deal with the collapse of the film: 'In the long run, we may end up doing what I did on *Beverly Hills Cop* and take it black.'

Interestingly, head of Columbia Pictures Mark Canton, and his second-in-command Barry Josephson, also laid claim to the idea of casting *Bad Boys* with black actors. Canton claimed he was desperate to do something with Will Smith after having seen *Six Degrees of Separation*, and *Bad Boys* seemed like ideal material. Keen to keep costs down, hiring a TV face like Will and pairing him with another TV star, black comedian Martin Lawrence, would allow Columbia to bring the film in for under $25 million.

For Will Smith, the leading role in *Bad Boys* was a sign of things to come. 'The significance of *Bad Boys* to me was that two black stars were in a film that was treated like a big-time film,' noted Will. 'Outside of Eddie Murphy and Whoopi Goldberg, you don't see this level of attention given to many films with black stars.' There were still worries about the project – Will knew that taking part in a Simpson-Bruckheimer action film would establish his presence in Hollywood, but without affording him the acting challenges he had enjoyed in *Six Degrees of Separation*. It was crunch time for Will Smith – he had to decide whether to put his desire for serious acting opportunities before his desire for success. Success won out. Once he had read the script, realising it was not the pale imitation of Eddie

Bad Boys was seen as a gamble, casting two relatively unknown actors (Will Smith and Martin Lawrence) in leading roles.

Murphy's *Beverly Hills Cop* he had feared, he signed on the dotted line. The Fresh Prince was now to be an action hero.

Becoming a movie action-hero meant some strenuous preparation for Will, very different from the drama tutorials and acting lessons for *Six Degrees of Separation*. He worked hard at putting muscles on his gangly, skinny frame, via a personal trainer, weight-lifting regimes, a strict personal diet and much time spent in the gym.

The on-screen chemistry between Martin Lawrence and Will Smith in Bad Boys *was immediate.*

The role of wildman-cop Mike Lowrey appealed to Will because it was another new departure, unlike either his previous TV or film roles. 'My role in *Bad Boys* is completely different from anything I have ever done. He is a playboy and I have never been a playboy,' he claimed, forgetting how close he had come during the first flush of success with his rap-music career. 'On screen and in real life,

I've always been the guy who couldn't get the girl. I like the change and I like the stretch. I went from *Fresh Prince* to *Six Degrees* and now to *Bad Boys*. I enjoy doing different things and trying to keep the audience off balance.'

Similarly appealing was the casting of his fellow TV sitcom star Martin Lawrence (of *The Martin Lawrence Show*) as family man Marcus Burnett. 'Working with Martin was great,' said Will. 'He's a comedic genius. We'd never worked together before, but it never felt like we were strangers – we got to really know each other. The chemistry was really great.'

Lawrence agreed. 'When I met Will, there was an immediate chemistry between us, and I knew that if we could get that on camera, we'd be cool,' he claimed. 'But we had a lot of fun. We worked hard together. Since both of us have comic timing on the sitcoms, we knew it was just a matter of getting together and finding out how we complemented each other.'

Despite the chemistry between the pair, *Bad Boys* was fraught with problems. The screenplay was subject to interminable redrafting, while the new-style action heroes had to draw on their own comedic talents to bring the film to life and provide laughs.

'We basically ad-libbed every scene,' Will claimed of their approach to making a film without a completed screenplay. 'It was two and a half months of two of the silliest guys in comedy doing exactly what they wanted to. That's the beauty of working with another comic. You go in in the morning and you have no clue what's about to happen. I'm used to changing lines on my show, and Martin does the same thing. It was like a tennis match. He would say something, then I'd toss a line right back.'

The production problems on *Bad Boys* were apparent to director Michael Bay from the beginning of the shoot, and he laid the blame at the door of producer Don Simpson. 'I watched my career go down the toilet the Saturday before shooting began,' claimed Bay, recalling how he had to begin shooting with an unfinished script. 'Don said, "We're taking our names off this project," while Jerry insisted, "Don't worry, we'll fix it." We would be shooting action sequences that should have taken four days to shoot, and we would have one.'

Rumours were rife during the production that turbulent producer Simpson had succumbed to his sex, drugs and rock 'n' roll lifestyle once more, after several periods in rehab. Contacted on set by *Los Angeles Magazine* writer Ed Dwyer, Simpson claimed a totally different addiction: 'It's true,' he said, 'I've fallen into a late-night pizza and M&M's pattern!' Despite the jokes, Simpson's 'livin' large' would catch up with him in a most spectacular way, when, in January 1996, he was found dead on the toilet of his Los Angeles home of a drug overdose during the production of the Nicolas Cage action film *The Rock*.

Such chaos could not unbalance Will, used as he was to improvising on his TV show, but it was a very different experience from the careful, controlled production of *Six Degrees of Separation.*

Part of the attraction of *Bad Boys*, however, was the chance to play cops and robbers. The film opens with Mike (Will) and Marcus (Martin Lawrence) celebrating a $100 million drugs bust in Miami. Their problems begin when the evidence is stolen from the police locker room and they are charged with recovering it. Along the way they tangle with murder witness Julie (Tea Leoni), get caught up in a case of mistaken identity and zoom through action set pieces and car chases.

'With all that jumping and shooting when you're making an action movie, you realise that it's a stunt, not a trick,' claimed Will. 'And it brings out all that testosterone. I saw how the situation brings that stuff out in people. Everybody has an action hero in them; everyone wants to kick in a door and shoot somebody.'

On the other hand, he noted, 'I knew it had to be as real as possible, because what makes you an effective superhero is that you don't want to be one. Like Bruce Willis in *Die Hard* – the last thing he wanted to do was run over that glass barefoot. People can't relate to a guy who just jumps in front of bullets.'

The Simpson-Bruckheimer formula – resurrected successfully for *Crimson Tide* (1996), *The Rock* and Will Smith's own *Enemy of the State* (1998) – triumphed once again as *Bad Boys* rocked the box office. Released in the US in May 1995 to mixed reviews, with a budget of only $20 million the film grossed $15.5 million over the opening weekend – a very good figure for a non-holiday movie released in the pre-summer blockbuster period, with no real star names featured.

Critically, the film drew rave reviews for Will Smith. *Entertainment Weekly* pointed out that 'Smith . . . holds the camera with his matinee-idol sexiness and his quicksilver delivery of lines. There's a spark of canniness in casting Lawrence and Smith against type. Smith the clean cut sitcom prince plays the swinging bachelor, and Lawrence, notorious for the raunchiness of his stand-up routines, is the devoted family man. Lawrence and Smith are winningly smooth comic actors.'

For *People* it was the mixture of comedy and action which appealed: 'The unfailingly ingratiating Smith glides through the movie . . . an actor with a refined sense of comedy. He is also physically imposing enough to pull off a serious action film.'

Rolling Stone saw past the pyrotechnics, claiming that the movie's success lay with the actors. 'The climatic shoot-out inside an airplane hanger, complete with a 727 blowing sky high, slides the film into overdrive. It's all special effects noise and nonsense, but we're not fooled. Lawrence and Smith are the real firecrackers.'

Although Martin Lawrence had gone into *Bad Boys* as the more prominent of the two co-stars, by the time the film was a hit – going on to gross a total of $140 million in the US and another $75 million abroad – it was Will Smith who truly shone. Despite this, during production there had been no rivalry. 'From day one we completely left everything open for the other guy,' Will claimed on the *Today* show. 'We never had a problem with that. It wasn't fighting for screen time.'

The relationship between the pair continued after *Bad Boys* had wrapped – a period in which Lawrence experienced personal problems such as several run-ins with the law. Will supported him by making a cameo appearance in the comic's next movie, *A Thin Line Between Love and Hate*, and claimed he would not hesitate to make a sequel to *Bad Boys* with Lawrence.

'I always said that the way to be the greatest movie star ever would be to combine Eddie Murphy, Tom Hanks and Arnold Schwarzenegger.'

There was one blip in their relationship, however. Will was upset that Martin Lawrence received top billing for *Bad Boys*, feeling that his star status meant he should have appeared first on the movie marquee. So strong was Will's contention that he eventually opted to sever ties with his management agency, International Creative Management, and switch to the all-powerful Creative Artists Agency instead. It may have seemed a petty concern to some, but it was to have important ramifications for Will Smith's star power. Having CAA in his corner enabled the actor to snag top billing in his next film: the alien-invasion ensemble epic, *Independence Day*.

For Will, the success of *Bad Boys* was the final piece in the Hollywood masterplan he had been constructing: 'I always said that the way to be the greatest movie star ever would be to combine Eddie Murphy, Tom Hanks and Arnold Schwarzenegger,' he claimed. He knew he had pinned down the comedic aspect through his years on *The Fresh Prince of Bel-Air*. His performance in *Six Degrees of Separation* had done much to win him a reputation as a serious actor. With *Bad Boys*, he had even managed to find an action-hero persona. 'Just that one scene,' said Will, 'where I'm running down the street with a gun, my shirt open, you know, just pure testosterone. That was the missing piece.' As a result of the film's success, Will's asking price per movie had soared to around five million dollars, putting him on the Hollywood A-list.

As a player in tinsletown, Will Smith now had all the accompaniments to go with his new status. His Los Angeles office was a family affair: his sister Ellen, trained as a cosmetologist, was now Will's receptionist; brother Harry worked as his chief financial officer, handling his income and investments. Additionally, Will's older sister Pam remained in Philadelphia running business interests that included an ice manufacturing company and a charitable foundation that funded local education projects. (One beneficiary of this was Jeff Townes, who returned to Philadelphia to manage a community music project financed by Will.)

'I have a huge ego, but I don't impose it on people. You have to have a big ego to be an actor.'

Will wanted his office décor to reflect his own personality – although the main room boasted the traditional executive desk, it also featured a line of baseball caps stuck to the wall. A big-screen TV was nestled in one corner, while the tangled joystick cords of a Sega video console hung down in front of it. A mini-stereo stood poised on a low table, surrounded by cassettes. On the walls were lines of gold and platinum DJ Jazzy Jeff and the Fresh Prince records.

With a solid following of admirers persisting throughout the musical, TV, and, now, film stages of his career, Will received a mountain of fan mail. Next to his gold and platinum discs Will would also display the artistic endeavours of his fans, including a huge painting of a very laid-back Will Smith by a fan from Miami.

Some fans who followed him from his days as a teen rapper were worried that his production capacity on *The Fresh Prince of Bel-Air,* and increasing muscle in Hollywood, meant that their ordinary guy from Philly had turned into a monster with an ego the size of his bank balance. Having been humbled once before, though, a disarmingly honest Will was wise to the trappings of success.

'I have a huge ego,' he happily admitted, 'but I don't impose it on people. You have to have a big ego to be an actor. But I have control over that, because I don't like how it feels when other people throw their weight around. That experience makes me struggle really hard not to impose myself on people for selfish reasons.'

Despite his rise to the top of the Hollywood tree, Will was determined to stay as level-headed as possible. The purpose of being successful in the entertainment media was, after all, to have fun. 'I like to be silly, make jokes, people enjoy that,' said Will, trying to analyse his own success as an all round entertainer. 'People generally have fun in my life. So when the camera's turned on I'm having fun and I think people can see that, people can feel that when they watch the movies.'

Will Smith edged nearer to Hollywood A-list status with Bad Boys.

What Will learned from *Bad Boys* was to keep his performance light. Playing likeable characters became a career aim, channelling his energy away from serious dramas like *Six Degrees of Separation* toward blockbuster entertainments. It was a disappointment to some, but Will had no qualms about pursuing the quickest route to success. 'I don't like stress. People have so much stress in their lives that it's kind of a breath of fresh air to just sit for an hour and a half and watch a movie of somebody who's just having fun. I enjoy life, I enjoy people. And people – black, white, Asian . . . or alien – enjoy that energy.'

The invaluable lessons learned from early success and financial ruin ensured that Will Smith, at the still-young age of 27 was ready for the second blast of fame that kicked in with *Bad Boys*. 'I was in the music business first, and it's really cut-throat and hard,' he reminisced. 'So I had my ups and downs. Had money, then was broke. I kinda got my footing together before I got into television and the film world. Because this type of attention can make you crazy.'

In the personal sphere, Will's rocky marriage to Sheree Zampino finally collapsed after three years, in 1995. The end came as a shock to Will, too wrapped up in his work to improve the situation. He claimed he never realised his marriage was in trouble until 'she filed for divorce. That was a very difficult period in my life. A lot of pain.'

It was not a mutual decision to divorce. Will later made it clear that, however bad things became, he would never have entertained the idea of splitting up his family.

'There's three things that you can give your child. You give them love, you give them knowledge, you give them discipline.'

Although Sheree was concerned for Trey, she had decided to leave Will to aggressively pursue his career without having to worry about working on the marriage also. In an attempt to avoid any negative press coverage, the couple announced their decision to divorce as soon as they had made it.

The hardest parts were breaking the news to Trey, and applying for joint custody of their son. 'It's not the perfect situation,' noted Will, 'but that's what life has dealt. We all make mistakes, and we have to find the good things out of it. What was a mistake for me created the most beautiful thing I've ever seen in my life.'

With the failure of his marriage, Trey was to become ever more central to Will's life as ironically his marital break-up gave Will a renewed determination to live up to early promises of being the perfect father. 'I think Sheree did me a favour,' he reflected on the consequences of divorce. 'I'm hugely family oriented. To me, a child being able to hear the thunder outside and to run and jump into bed with his mother and father – I remember that from Philly. That's a memory my son will never have. There's still a pain that I feel, that my son will never experience some of the beauty that I experienced of having a family. There's almost a kind of weird guilt.'

Time spent with his son became precious, now that Trey was splitting his time equally between father and mother. 'There's three things that you can give your child,' Will claimed. 'You give them love, you give them knowledge, you give them discipline. You give your kids those three things, and everything else is in the hands of the Lord.'

Despite Sheree's conviction that Will's obsessive working habits and commitment to his career had broken up their marriage, Will put the blame on their mutually young ages. 'I had no business getting married,' he admitted. 'Neither one of us were ready. We hadn't experienced enough life yet to be together. When you don't know enough about yourself, you can't know someone else.'

Sheree was forced to agree. 'We were young,' she said, 'but we have a beautiful baby. Everything is cool – it worked out.'

'Trey has a mommy and a daddy and there are two separate houses and that's just what his life is,' conceded Will. 'It isn't the optimum situation, but that's his reality. I think a child having both parents is much more important [than fighting over the divorce].'

Sheree reputedly walked off with a one-million-dollar cash settlement, around $24,000 each month in alimony and child support and a trust fund for Trey's education later in life. It was an expensive way to avoid a fight, but Will had put his son's interests before his own and, as a result of his burgeoning career, the millionaire star could afford it.

Despite his public show of goodwill, Will was traumatised by the divorce. If he had his own way, he would have happily continued in the relationship until Trey was significantly older – even if things were not working out. That was not enough to satisfy Sheree Zampino. When asked about her response when Will suggested staying together for Trey's sake despite their difficulties, he replied: 'She thought it was the most ridiculous thing in the world.'

As a child of divorced parents himself, Will felt that the big split was the first real failure in his life. 'I made a lot of mistakes in those days,' he candidly admitted later. 'What aggravated things was the death of my infant half-brother, Sterling, which occurred during that time and took me back to Philadelphia. I intend to spend more time there with my family.'

06
BOOM! SHAKE THE ROOM

Will Smith's growing presence on the big screen left him with a difficult decision to make. It was time to say goodbye to *The Fresh Prince* once and for all.

'I felt like it was time to end the show,' he told *Ebony* magazine. 'We had a nice run. I had done movies like *Six Degrees of Separation* and *Bad Boys*, I was up for more – including *Independence Day* – and the TV show just felt confining. You're pretty much one character, and there are not many peaks and valleys, just the same old, same old. I wanted to go out while we were still good. You get up to eight or nine seasons and then you're struggling. I wanted to go out while we were still funny.'

Will still had to break the news to the cast, crew, writers and producers that the sixth season – running through 1995 to 1996 – would be the last. He was only too aware that many people, both in front of and behind the scenes, relied on the show for their incomes, but felt he had stuck with it for long enough. Ever since making *Six Degrees of Separation*, he had felt increasingly limited by each successive season of *The Fresh Prince of Bel-Air*. Loyalty to the production team, cast and crew had kept him on the show for two restless years, as had his increasing power behind the scenes.

Will's desire to leave the show had been evident for some time, so his decision was hardly a surprise to all concerned. 'Artistically, the show has made me somewhat crazed,' he admitted prior to quitting. 'But I'll stick with it through to the end of my contract. When I got into this business, the most important thing for me was to always stay on the edge. It's really difficult with television to be anywhere near the edge, especially Monday night at 8pm!'

Will's attempts to beef up the show, by introducing topics like drugs, sex, prejudice and inner-city tension, had gone some way toward retaining his interest. However, much of this material had sat uneasily in a show that boasted such mainstream guest stars over its six-year run as chat show queen Oprah Winfrey, *Star Trek*'s William Shatner, Jay Leno, Will's mentor Quincy Jones, musicians Tom Jones and B. B. King and actresses Robin Givens and Vanessa Williams.

Everyone was given fair warning of Will's plans. For him, it was getting harder and harder to play the part of the naive street kid from Philly when so much had changed in his own life. 'It became increasingly difficult to find that guy inside me,' claimed Will. 'All the things the Fresh Prince stood for, all the fun he had, still exist inside me, it's just that those aren't the dominant aspects of my personality anymore.'

'When I started, I was twenty years old. Inside those six years, I went through three careers – music, television, movies. I got married, had a baby, divorced. It's like I did a whole lot of living in that time. My life experiences are so far advanced beyond the character's life experiences, it was almost like a regression for me to play the character.'

The hardest part for Will was leaving behind those people on the show he counted as close friends. The major cast members had even accompanied Will on holiday early in the series' run. 'The thing about that show is that it's a family,' he asserted as everything drew to a close. 'We had a ball. The people start to take on the surrogate roles of the characters, you start to have those kind of concerns for the people that you work with. It's like leaving a family, more than just leaving a job. But creatively, I was starting to feel stagnant; there wasn't anywhere to go. I had seen how vast the film world could be. You can do anything on a big screen, there's so much more room. That was more exciting.'

Will also wanted to make sure the series came to a proper conclusion, rather than being cancelled after going on too long as with many other American TV shows. When actor Sherman Hemsley – best know as George Jefferson on the long-running *The Jeffersons* sitcom – did a guest spot on *The Fresh Prince*, he told Will he was doing the right thing. 'He said the way that they found out that *The Jeffersons* was over is they came to the set one Monday, and their parking spaces were gone,' related Will. 'You know, I don't want to go out that way. They never had a final episode. You need to close that chapter in your life. I wanted to plan the going out. You know, go out standing, rather than go out on your back.'

Will got his way. After six years and 149 half-hour instalments, the final episode of *The Fresh Prince of Bel-Air* was transmitted on 20 May 1996. Recording that episode had been an emotional rollercoaster for Will, and it was followed by an outrageous wrap party which, in true Fresh Prince prankster style, soon descended into a frantic food fight between the cast.

'I like the genre of the "big-budget-Hollywood-blow 'em up-shoot 'em up" movies. That's fun for me. It's physical.'

Although at heart a feel-good comedy, Will was proudest of those episodes that managed to raise issues that its teenaged audience was dealing with in real life, even if it was from within the safe environment of the rich Banks family's home. 'From the fan mail I've received, I know the show helped many teens get through difficult situations,' claimed Will of his time on the sitcom. 'Even if we couldn't offer them solutions, our show had shown them that they're not alone.'

The creator of the show and Will's personal manager, Benny Medina, was aware that, however blasé his star appeared, Will was upset to be severing his ties. 'He was dazed in a way,' Medina recalled. 'He had this kind of look I've seen when something deep is going on, but he doesn't want to let on what's going on for fear it'll cause someone else to become emotional. I was probably the first person to see him after he did his last scene for the series. He walks through the empty house and then leaves. I saw him come off the set and his eyes were full of tears.'

When Will Smith was offered one of the leading roles in a science fiction film, *Independence Day*, he recognised it as an opportunity not to be missed. 'It was one of those projects that comes along once in a career. It has everything. You laugh, you cry, and it has action. It has an ensemble cast. It's everything you could want from a movie. I'm also probably the first black guy to ever save the world.'

Having switched from TV to film, from the serious drama of *Six Degrees of Separation* to the action-adventure of *Bad Boys*, Will Smith was about to make another career departure. 'I'm really drawn to it,' he said of the screenplay's genre. 'I like doing science fiction. I like action. I like the genre of the "big-budget-Hollywood-blow 'em up-shoot 'em up" movies. That's fun for me. It's physical.'

Behind the simple 'What if . . . ?' premise of *Independence Day* were director Roland Emmerich and writer Dean Devlin, who had made the low-budget SF films *Moon 44, Universal Soldier* and *Stargate*. Pure sci-fi hokum, they had nonetheless drawn loyal audiences world-wide. Now Emmerich and Devlin were moving into the big time, with a big budget from 20th Century Fox and a series of respected names (Bill Pullman, Jeff Goldblum, Robert Loggia) for the ultimate alien invasion movie.

The origins of *Independence Day* – often referred to as *ID4*, an allusion to the Fourth of July (American Independence Day) – were simple. According to Emmerich, he wondered how people would genuinely react if an alien spacecraft appeared above their city one morning. 'What would really happen in your life?' mused the German-born director. 'In all our lives? What kind of direction would everything take? What great moments those are for a film-maker to put on film. I thought, why isn't anybody doing a new version of *War of the Worlds*?'

Mixing the best elements of countless SF movies from the fifties with state-of-the-art special effects and an offbeat sense of humour, Emmerich and Devlin conceived a David-and-Goliath style confrontation between the invading aliens and defending earthlings. Among the latter group was US Air Force Captain Steven Hiller – the part played by Will Smith.

One of Will's Hollywood ambitions was finally coming true. The central character of *ID4* was not written as race specific – by pure chance, a black actor was cast as the central hero of what would become one of the biggest blockbuster movies of all time. 'It wasn't intentional,' admitted Emmerich. 'It wasn't written like that, I talked to Will and he said, "The script has no reference to it. Should we reference it?" I said, "No, because you are a hero, period. It has nothing to do with your colour, race or religion."'

This was the Hollywood breakthrough Will Smith had been waiting for all his acting career. Emmerich knew from Will's previous work that he was ideal for the role of the light-hearted but full-blooded fighter-pilot character: 'We knew from *Fresh Prince* that he could be funny and we knew from *Six Degrees of Separation* that he could be serious.'

For Emmerich, it was a straightforward decision to avoid the standard Hollywood hero types like Tom Cruise, Chris O'Donnell or Brad Pitt. 'I simply cast Will because I think he's the best young hero out there,' Emmerich claimed. 'I believe he's one of the biggest rising stars. Sometimes you see an actor and you know what's happening. I thought the same thing when I saw Brad Pitt in *Thelma and Louise*. It's amazing how the *ID4* audience immediately overcomes who he was before and totally accept what he's doing.'

Will talked of his role in Independence Day *as being 'the first black guy ever to save the world.'*

Preparing to play an action hero who saves the Earth, Will looked to his Hollywood predecessors for inspiration. 'Bruce Willis and Harrison Ford really showed me how to play this character,' admitted Will. As a big fan of the *Star Wars* movies, he was very familiar with Ford's heroic role as intergalactic outlaw Han Solo. He was also keen to emulate Bruce Willis's succesful switch from TV star to movie hero. 'Willis plays heroes who don't want to be heroes. Ford kind of plays his heroes that way, too. That was the one thing that I really concentrated on: don't be the guy who walks out with the gun in his hand and stands in the middle of the room, shooting away while everyone is shooting all around him. I want to be the guy who says, "Why are you all shooting at me?" I want to be the guy who does the heroic things out of necessity, not out of enjoyment of it.'

Will's pre-planned formula – combining the humour of Eddie Murphy, the nice guy appeal of Tom Hanks and the action man credentials of a Schwarzenegger or Willis – provided him with a movie persona which would captivate audiences world-wide. As ever, he was very carefully re-tracing the footsteps of those who had gone down the same route before him. 'I studied what happened to Tom Hanks, Robin Williams and Eddie Murphy. In the earlier days, people didn't trust the TV-to-movies transition. Eddie Murphy was the person I really watched, just to see how the transition is made. The acting difference is subtle. The film screen is much bigger, you have to do less. On TV everything in performance is "big", so

Will with singer/actor Harry Connick Jr. in Independence Day.

you have to pull back on film.'

The production process of a big screen blockbuster proved daunting to Will Smith – he soon learned, for example, that the working methods of Don Simpson, who began shooting *Bad Boys* without a finalised script, were far from unique. Unfazed, Will threw himself into a period of research to ensure believability in his role of a jet-fighter pilot. Studying the basics of flying an F-16 with a Marine lieutenant, he also persuaded the military to allow him to try out their state-of-the-art flight simulators.

Another whole new series of challenges awaited Will Smith during the production of *ID4*. While some of the action scenes may have seemed vaguely familiar from the making of *Bad Boys*, he had the added challenge of acting against numerous explosions, stunts and special-effects aliens. One particularly hard-to-achieve scene turned out to be one of the most memorable in the film, when Captain Hiller goes *mano-a-mano* with an alien creature after crash landing in the desert.

The scene was filmed in Utah on the notorious Bonneville Salt Flats. It was an experience etched in Will's memory. 'That was worse than the desert,' he complained. 'The sun was ten times hotter and the days were longer. You don't know what you're doing because everything is special effects and I was out there with the alien. They tell you, "The alien will be behind you." That was a little difficult, trying to find the performance with none of the elements there. A good 70 per cent of my stuff in the movie is me by myself, so I could do what I felt in those scenes.'

'Flying the alien spacecraft was very strange. I did all of it sitting in a chair. There was nothing, so I was just trying to feel the scene.'

Will found the whole process basically disorientating. 'If you're acting with an alien, it's a mark on the floor or something. And it's [filmed] in such small pieces you can never really get a good run at a scene,' he said. 'So it's difficult finding the moments. But what's fun about doing a science fiction movie is when you finally see everything put together, it's almost as if you weren't even there. It looks completely different. On the set, they'll say, "Okay, look to the left and just say your line to the left," and you're like, "What the heck is that for?" But when you see it all together it's amazing.'

Will was forced to exercise his imagination in an entirely new way. Used to working with real people and real props, he had to work hard to make an impact among *ID4's* five hundred special-effects shots. 'Flying the alien spacecraft was very strange,' he noted. 'I did all of it sitting in a chair. There was nothing, so I was just trying to feel the scene. What was great about Dean [Devlin, writer] and Roland [Emmerich, director] was that they knew exactly what they wanted. They were so clear that I had a picture of what they wanted. But there were so many elements that weren't there that I felt almost helpless.'

Much more enjoyable, from Will's point of view, was his work with the real flesh-and-blood cast – primarily Jeff Goldblum, with whom he is teamed up for much of the climax of the film. In fact, they hit it off so well during location shoots that they occasionally found it difficult to take their own acting seriously. 'It was just one of those bizarre nights,' recalled Will of one incident with Goldblum. 'It was about midnight and we had been there all day. Now we were expected to save the world. It was really bizarre because everything was hilarious. The seriousness of saving the world became hilarious. We got into this laughing jag that doubled us over. Life as we knew it depended on Jeff Goldblum and Will Smith! I turned to Jeff and said: "Man, this planet is in trouble. Give up now! Surrender!" It got to be so funny that we were looking at each other and cracking up saying, "Who the hell would pick you to save the world? You were *The Fly*, for God's sake!"'

At the heart of Will's attraction to the film, however, was his character, wise-cracking family man and Marine pilot Steven Hiller. 'He's interesting because he's definitely serious, but he's also able to be funny,' noted Will. 'I've never experimented with that before. It's either been one or the other.' This mix of drama and comedy would be integral in developing a Will Smith movie persona that would soon become known the whole world over.

The summer of 1996 belonged to *Independence Day*, which overshadowed a whole slew of would-be blockbusters – including *Twister*, *The Rock* – which teamed Nicolas Cage with Sean Connery – and Tom Cruise in *Mission: Impossible*. The Fourth of July – Independence Day itself – was D-Day for the film as it opened nation-wide on 2400 screens. Over the first five days of release, taking in the holiday weekend, the film grossed $83.5 million, making it the highest grossing film over a five-day period to that date. By the sixth day, the box office take was just shy of $96 million and within two months, the film was heading towards $300 million, second only to Steven Spielberg's *Jurassic Park* (1992) in the speed of its phenomenal box-office gross. The world-wide reaction was the same, with record-breaking weekend openings bringing in an international box-office gross of $800 million. It was an extremely impressive return on a film with a budget of $71 million – which was relatively low for a film featuring so many special effects.

For Will Smith, the effect was immediate. Acquainted with fame via his various incarnations in music, TV and as a movie action hero in *Bad Boys*, he was still not fully prepared for the attention that came his way as soon as *ID4* opened. 'What happened with *Independence Day* was really weird,' he remembered. 'I was in New York the weekend that it opened [shooting *Men in Black*] and on the Wednesday and Thursday of that week people would drive by going "Hey, Will how you doing?", screaming "Good to see you, Will, what's up?" That Monday after *Independence Day* opened, people on the street were like, "Mr Smith, hello, it's really good to see you. Congratulations on everything." And I was like, "Whoa, that movie is big!"'

Will mixed serious acting with straight comedy for his role in Independence Day *to good effect, creating a unique persona for himself that would lay the basis for future roles.*

Later in 1996, cinema exhibitors also recognised Will Smith's contribution to the success of *ID4* by giving him the International Box Office Achievement of the Year Award. Will himself attributed the world-wide impact of the movie down to director Roland Emmerich's European sensibility, which looked at America from outside. 'Well, that's the thing about the movie, it's not really an American blockbuster,' he claimed. 'In the film, we as a planet are about to be annihilated and if we can't put our prejudices – our racism and sexism and all our "isms" – behind us, then we will all be destroyed. So interestingly enough, the movie is about a unification of the entire world.'

Prominent critic Roger Ebert, of the *Chicago Sun-Times*, took the film less seriously, noting that '*Independence Day* is in the tradition of silly summer fun, and on that level I kind of liked it, as, indeed, I kind of like any movie with the courage to use the line, "It's the end of the world as we know it."'

It was over a year after his divorce from Sheree Zampino before Will Smith struck up a new relationship. This time, he was not getting to know someone from scratch, or making the mistake of falling in love on the rebound – the new love of his life was a long-time friend, actress Jada Pinkett. The pair had known each other for seven years, but it was not until 1996 that a romance developed between them.

Will first met Jada when she auditioned for the role as his TV girlfriend on *The Fresh Prince of Bel-Air* in 1990. Though the producers turned her down – as she was only five feet tall, compared to Will's six foot three inches – the pair had remained in touch over the years. However, it was only in the wake of Will's divorce that Jada got a second chance to audition for the role of his love interest – this time in real life. 'Jada Pinkett is my best friend,' Will gently asserted, 'and when you can combine your best friend in the world with the person who is also your lover and your partner, there is an emotional and spiritual and physical ecstasy that is unmatched.'

Born in Baltimore on 18 September 1971, Jada was three years younger than Will. She enjoyed a similar background to her Fresh Prince, her father working as a contractor and her mother as a nurse. As a natural performer, she pursued a professional acting career from an early age, training at the Baltimore School of the Arts and the North Carolina School of the Arts. Like Will, she had also gone to Hollywood to win a role in a sitcom, *A Different World*. (Ironically, it was on the set of *A Different World* that Will had met his first wife, Sheree Zampino.)

Despite being younger, Jada had enjoyed an earlier start in movies than Will with roles in *Menace II Society* (1993), *Jason's Lyric* (1994, as the title character Lyric), the *Tales from the Crypt* movie *Demon Knight* (1995), *The Nutty Professor* remake (1996), co-starring with Will's idol Eddie Murphy, and girl-gang heist movie *Set it Off* (1996).

As Will's marriage was falling apart in the second half of 1995, it was to Jada Pinkett that he turned for advice as a friend. 'I helped him understand what had happened in his marriage,' Jada said of their developing romance, 'and he helped me see what had happened in my relationships. He's become my best friend. There's nothing I can't say to him, nothing I can't share. He's smart, spiritual, sensitive.'

At the time, Jada was just a shoulder for Will to cry on. She was also able to provide the advice and support he needed to set things straight after his split with Sheree. 'She's very in touch with her emotions, which allows me to be in touch with mine,' he said of the woman who would become his wife and Trey's step-mother. 'She helps me deal with everything I have to deal with. She makes everything okay. No matter how difficult it gets, she always has something kind to say or a warm hug.'

'The beauty of life with Jada is that . . . she understands fame, she understands fans, having money, not having money and how that affects you psychologically and emotionally. She understands what I do.'

Will found he never had to explain or make excuses to Jada for time devoted to his acting career – she was in the exact same position herself. 'Actors hook up out of necessity,' claimed Will as their friendship changed to romance. 'The beauty of life with Jada is that what happened with my first marriage wouldn't make Jada panic. She understands that place, she understands fame, she understands fans, having money, not having money and how that affects you psychologically and emotionally. She understands what I do.'

Other people were also beginning to understand what Will Smith could do – post-*Independence Day,* many top Hollywood movie directors were eager to work with him. Receiving a call from someone claiming to be Steven Spielberg while relaxing at home, Will assumed the person was playing a prank. 'I'd just finished *Independence Day* and I'm hanging out in my underwear,' he recalled. 'When I realised it wasn't a joke, I started dressing and tidying up my apartment while he's on the phone, because, you know, this is the Man!'

07

JUST THE TWO OF US

'This ain't no Steven Spielberg. You don't even sound like Steven Spielberg!' That was how Will Smith welcomed the crank caller who had got hold of his personal phone number and claimed to be the director of *Jaws, Close Encounters of the Third Kind, ET* and *Jurassic Park*. 'Stop playing with me. Who is this?' Embarrassment started to creep in as the voice at the other end of the phone asserted, with solid authority, 'This *is* Steven, Will.'

For the 28-year-old actor, this was a moment he had dreamt of. Will had long looked forward to a time when audiences would regard a black actor in the same way as they would Tom Cruise or Brad Pitt. Those days seemed to be getting nearer. 'It makes you feel special when Steven Spielberg calls you at home . . .' testified Will.

The call from Spielberg was to lead Will Smith into another SF blockbuster movie, his second film to dominate the box office over the Independence Day

Will described his second wife Jada Pinkett as keeping him utterly grounded in reality.

holiday weekend. 'That's my weekend – July Fourth. I own that,' claimed Will when it became clear that his second holiday hit, *Men in Black* (1997), was almost as big as *Independence Day*.

Spielberg was calling in his capacity as executive producer of *Men in Black*, a screenplay which had been in development since 1992, based on a cult comic book. The comic book, created by Lowell Cunningham, with its premise of ultra-cool FBI-type agents battling aliens on earth, was snapped up by Spielberg's production company, Amblin. The plan was to have the film on screen by 1994 – so confident were the producers that they had personal sweatshirts made declaring, 'In 1994 They're Coming', just before the film got trapped in production hell.

'There were probably two different versions of the script that we developed internally before we got to this story,' explained Spielberg of the five-year period it took to bring *Men in Black* to the screen. 'We spoke to Barry Sonnenfeld about it and ended up waiting for him to get through *Get Shorty*. The movie required a very particular tone that few directors could have brought, and Barry was at the top of the list.'

Sonnenfeld had started life as a cinematographer, responsible for some of the wilder shots in the Coen brothers' first three films, *Blood Simple* (1984), *Raising Arizona* (1987) and *Miller's Crossing* (1990). He made his directorial debut with *The Addams Family* (1991), updating the popular 1960's TV series and perfectly capturing the work of macabre cartoonist Charles Addams, following it with *Addams Family Values* (1995).

As soon as he read the screenplay, Sonnenfeld knew that *Men in Black* was right up his street. 'I loved its sensibility because I've always believed deeply that we as humans really don't have a clue about what's going on,' he claimed. 'I loved the fact that I could make a movie, play it for the reality of the situation, with aliens in it.'

The story was finally focussed on world-weary MiB (Men in Black) Agent K (Tommy Lee Jones), who is paired with NYPD officer James Edwards, known as Agent J (Will Smith). Together with pathologist Laura Weaver (Linda Fiorentino) they have to hunt down and eradicate a bug-like alien called Edgar (Vincent D'Onofrio) who is out to assassinate a couple of otherworldly ambassadors. Along the way, a whole host of weird and wonderful aliens living secretly on earth are encountered.

The first actor to be cast was the notoriously difficult Tommy Lee Jones – who confirmed his reputation by trying to have the film recast as a vehicle for him alone, as the one and only Man in Black. 'They started out as caustic but intelligent complaints,' recalled Sonnenfeld of Jones' concerns. 'Like, "This isn't funny, this isn't real" and by the end became, "Why men in black? Why the black?"

You know, it was like, Why not throw out everything?' Scathing about the screenplay, Jones was also wary about repeating the bad experience of *Batman Forever*, where he was overshadowed by Jim Carrey as his over-acting, scene-stealing comedy sidekick. 'I knew Tommy didn't want that to happen again,' confirmed Sonnenfeld.

Three additional screenwriters rewrote the original screenplay by Ed Solomon (who had launched Keanu Reeves' career with *Bill and Ted's Excellent Adventure* [1990]), including *Jurassic Park* writer David Koepp. Once they had a script which dealt with most of Jones' concerns, the production was ready to go full steam ahead.

'Ninety per cent of making a movie is the team. You can't beat that team.'

Sonnenfeld and Spielberg were clear about who they wanted to team up with straight character actor Tommy Lee Jones. They needed someone lighter, with good comic timing and the ability to draw a crowd to the movie over the opening weekend. After the success of *Bad Boys* and *Independence Day,* there was really only one choice. However, when the producers first approached Will Smith he was still tied up with *The Fresh Prince of Bel-Air*. Alternatives were considered, including Chris O'Donnell (who had won out over Will for the part of Robin in *Batman Forever*) and Brad Pitt, but no one truly seemed to fit. Fortunately, by the time the film was ready to roll Will was free of his TV commitments. 'He's a totally honest actor,' observed Steven Spielberg of his favoured co-star. 'He's funny and he's serious, all rolled into one . . .'

For his part, Will now knew with certainty that he had become a player in the industry. 'I think that the combination of *Six Degrees of Separation* and *Bad Boys* kind of showed Hollywood, "Okay, this guy can pretty much do anything we throw at him,"' he asserted self-assuredly. Nonetheless, there was a small seed of doubt implanted in his mind: did he really want to repeat himself so soon? 'I was a little concerned about doing two alien movies back-to-back,' he confided of his fear that *Men in Black* might be looked upon as *Independence Day 2,* 'but when Steven Spielberg calls you at home what are you supposed to say?'

Besides, the chance to star opposite Tommy Lee Jones in a Spielberg-produced movie was too much to resist, even if it meant more blue screen work with nonexistent aliens. 'Ninety per cent of making a movie is the team,' acknowledged Will. 'You can't beat that team, so I was in.' After all, when he had analysed the elements that made up the most successful films of all time, he found that 'creatures' – whether aliens, dinosaurs or sharks – had featured prominently in them all. *Men in Black* had blockbuster written all over it.

Special effects and cinematic spectacle aside, however, Will had a definite empathy with the role of Agent J. 'J is the kind of character who enjoys life and experiencing new things,' he explained. 'He also thinks he's the smartest person in the world, so becoming an MiB is the ultimate challenge.'

Will's biggest personal challenge was to avoid simply repeating the role of Captain Steven Hiller from *Independence Day* as if he were an NYPD officer instead of a Marine. Whereas his previous roles had all been very different from each other, now he was playing his second consecutive light-hearted alien-fighter. 'I felt comfortable with that because you change everything for the character,' he claimed. 'There are subtle differences with the Marine, you know. In *Independence Day*, you have the shoulders back, you're standing up. The whole posture, and the walk, and the attitude, and all of that stuff is completely different. Whereas with the *Men in Black* character, how he sits in a chair, and the whole attitude, is that New York cop kind of thing. The central similarities that I like to bring to characters is the fun.'

Principal photography began in March 1996, with an eighteen-week production schedule taking in location shoots in Los Angeles and Manhattan and studio filming across five sound-stages at Sony Pictures in LA. Pre-production had already been underway for over a year, with Oscar-winning creature-creator Rick Baker hard at work developing the aliens – including Edgar the Bug and Mikey, who appears in the opening sequence.

As with *Independence Day*, Will soon found himself acting against invisible co-stars. 'I'm an expert now, but special-effects work is so tedious. It's difficult to get a performance because it's so technical. You have to get your head a certain way, then your arm has to be up a certain way when you're talking to the alien. It's like, aargh! And it's one line at a time. You gotta pay so much attention to saying it at the right tempo, and at the right time, that you can't concentrate on being normal.

'When you get into a movie, especially a special effects movie, the tempo is so much slower. Someone will put something there with an X on it and that's the alien for today. It's difficult to try and get the emotion. Every frame of film has to be set perfectly. While you're shooting, they play around with it; like Barry Sonnenfeld would kind of explain things to you, "Okay, this alien is big and he's going to go, Aaaargh!, that's what he's going to do." And I was like, "Thanks a lot, Barry."'

Will Smith and Tommy Lee Jones in Men in Black. *Will described his co-star as 'a riot'.*

Despite his co-star's difficult reputation, and his initial unwillingness to share *Men in Black* as a buddy movie, Will Smith got along surprisingly well with Tommy Lee Jones. 'It's really weird. We had a ball on the set of this movie,' said Will. 'I know it might be hard to believe, but Tommy Lee Jones is actually a comedic genius. He really understands comedy to a technical level that very few people understand. Deadpan delivery is the most difficult, but he can do it because he does nothing: he just says the words. For me that's perfect. We called it "soft pitching". And with that dead-straight delivery, he would toss me soft pitches, that I could smack out of the ballpark. Just lobbin' those jokes up there for me.'

Will Smith and Tommy Lee Jones found that working together on set was a real blast, complimenting each other's style in the process.

Will found himself paying great attention to the way Tommy Lee Jones approached his work. Aware he had won an Oscar for best supporting actor in the film *The Fugitive* (1993) and had made his directorial debut with *The Good Old Boys*, featuring rising star Matt Damon, 'The one thing that I really picked up from him during shooting is that he knows about everything on set,' noted Will. 'He knows how the cameras work, how the lights work, he knows all the technical aspects of every job on the set, in order to be able to put himself in a position to have his brilliance captured. So I really started paying attention to a lot of those things this time around.' At the back of his mind, Will Smith may have been preparing for the day he himself would take the helm behind the cameras.

For his part, Tommy Lee Jones came to be similarly appreciative of Will. 'Will is double-cool,' he appraised. 'I just hoped I could keep up with him in the cool department.'

So good did the rapport become between the two stars that they both made it clear they would be willing to team up for a sequel. Will also came to believe that the older actor's difficult reputation had been unfairly attached to him: 'Well, the thing about Tommy Lee Jones is that he's a perfectionist. He's won an Oscar and all of that, so there is a certain air he carries and people make themselves uncomfortable around him. I found that, that's Tommy Lee. He's kind of really quiet and strong looking, so you make yourself uncomfortable. Also his sense of humour is so different. People don't know how to take it, he throws people off balance with it. He's a riot.'

Will's good-natured analysis of his screen partner found an echo in people who were, in fact, made uncomfortable by him. 'Outside Will's trailer were all these eight-year-old kids who watched *Fresh Prince*,' recalled co-star Linda Fiorentino. 'He was like the Pied Piper. Nobody was outside Tommy's trailer. Everybody was afraid of him.'

Will became the hero of the *Men in Black* set, simply by maintaining his relaxed yet professional attitude over long days of complicated filming. 'Will on the set is incredibly relaxed, self-confident and at ease with himself,' noted Barry Sonnenfeld. 'He's always energetic, bouncing on his toes. He's just got too much energy.'

After a difficult and lengthy gestation, it seemed inevitable that *Men in Black* should suffer a crisis during shooting. Halfway through making the movie, director Sonnenfeld summed it up as a 'sci-fi action-comedy with no action, no adventure and no ending'. Even creating the variety of creatures had not been without its problems. Sonnenfeld observed of the Edgar Bug character, created for the climax, 'It was a great looking monster for talking, but it wasn't designed to move.'

This resulted in a request to Steven Spielberg to extend the special effects budget by $2.5 million. 'It's hard because I'm basically directing two movies,' admitted Sonnenfeld, whose misgivings over the scenes requiring Edgar Bug to move would be cancelled out by special computer techniques created by Industrial Light and Magic.

These same scenes resulted in Will's lowest point during the making of the film. 'The goo was the worst day,' he explained of the slime that covered him and

Tommy Lee Jones as the bug exploded. 'It was glycerine mixed with some kind of food particles to make it look chunky. You could actually eat the stuff. They needed something that could get in your nose and mouth. You could lick yourself clean. It was terribly disgusting. Those were the two most difficult days making the movie.'

Even prior to the film's opening, Will predicted big things for *Men in Black*. 'This is balls out comedy,' he enthused. 'From the beginning, this movie is just fun. It can be really silly and it can be really smart, you know? There's a lot of different colour and angles. This is the type of movie that will mark points in people's lives. I remember the day *Star Wars* came out. That's the kind of movie *Men in Black* is, it's going to inspire the next Spielberg who is only nine years old. It's going to inspire people to take things to the next level. There's digital work in this movie that you've just never seen anything like before.'

'I'm getting more calls from people who have faith in my abilities. It just makes you feel good that big studios are willing to bank on you for their big movie of the summer.'

Will was now playing the Hollywood game of waiting for the opening weekend's box office figures, for the third time in a row. In 1995, *Bad Boys* had been a surprise hit, while the scale of success enjoyed by *Independence Day* in 1996 had come as a complete shock. Now he was ready for the Fourth of July weekend release of *Men in Black* – even if he did not approve of the Hollywood custom of predicting a film's total box-office gross based on its first few days' takings. 'I hate those opening weekends,' he admitted. 'I try not to pay attention to the box office. Just do the work. Enjoy it if it's a good movie, and you're happy with your work. Let that be enough. To have to earn $100 million in seventeen minutes is too much pressure, and it is really out of your control.'

Will need not have worried. Over the six-day holiday period *Men in Black* took $84.1 million, falling just $12 million shy of the same period's box-office gross for *Independence Day*. After eight weeks on release the take amounted to $220 million, with a further $313 million world-wide making *Men in Black* the highest earning movie of 1997.

The overwhelmingly positive reviews undoubtedly helped the film hit the heights. 'A lot of big-budget special-effects films are on the wrong side of self-parody and don't know it. *Men in Black* knows it and glories in it,' said Roger Ebert in the *Chicago Sun-Times*. For *USA Today*, *Men in Black* was '*Independence Day* for smart people . . . Smith is so appealingly cool, it should be illegal.' According to the *San Francisco Chronicle*, 'Smith's best qualities as a comic actor emerge' in *Men in Black*.

Will's comic persona was allowed to dominate throughout Men in Black.

The effect of *Men in Black* on Will Smith's career cannot be underestimated. Following *Independence Day*, it put him in the same bracket as those major Hollywood stars whose status he had aspired to, such as Tom Hanks, Harrison Ford and Tom Cruise. 'Before *Men in Black*, I wasn't the first or second or 38th choice for this type of movie,' Will admitted. 'I'm getting more calls from people who have faith in my abilities. It just makes you feel good that big studios are willing to bank on you for their big movie of the summer.'

After a four-year absence from the music scene since 1993, due to falling record sales (his last album, *Code Red*, had only sold 300,000 copies in 1993) and the pressure of his film and TV work, Will Smith used *Men in Black* as an opportunity to get back behind the microphone. This time he was recording in his own right, without DJ Jazzy Jeff as back-up, but with a blockbuster movie theme as a foolproof launch pad.

'Jada is completely real; she's comfortable with the press and the attention. She really keeps me in a grounded place.'

The two songs he contributed to the soundtrack – 'Men in Black' and 'Just Cruisin'' – immediately stormed the charts around the world. Although he had begun to think of his music career in the past tense, such was the success of these recordings that he was offered a lucrative recording deal with Columbia Records – another offer that Will just could not refuse.

The video to promote 'Men in Black' allowed Will to have further fun with the image initially created for the film. 'The alien could dance,' he said of his computer-generated video co-star. 'This *Men in Black* thing has really just opened my life up. I'm letting that inner child run free.'

Things were also going well in Will's personal life. Despite being away from Trey while shooting *Men in Black*, his absences did not have the same effect on Jada Pinkett as they previously had on Sheree Zampino. As an actress herself she too had been busy with her own roles in films, as well as directing music videos for a variety of bands. 'Jada has a special understanding,' said Will of the woman who would become his second wife. 'She's reality. Jada is completely real; she's comfortable with the press and the attention. She really keeps me in a grounded place: that life is really the most important thing, and how a big movie, and all of that, is fun. You can enjoy that, and Hollywood premieres, but your life and your family is what's really important.'

For her part, Jada recognised the same understanding and sympathetic qualities in Will. 'Our lives are so parallel,' she said, 'our ideas, our philosophies –

everything just matches. I cannot imagine being on this planet with anybody else.'

Having committed to getting married before the end of the year, Will Smith and Jada Pinkett made it with a few hours to spare – holding their private wedding ceremony on 31 December, 1997, at a mansion called Cloisters, just outside Jada's hometown of Baltimore, Maryland. Around 125 guests were invited to the wedding, but – in an effort to keep the press away – they were driven to the secret location in black limousines with no idea of where they were actually going.

The event cost in excess of three million dollars – a figure now easily afforded by Will, who could command around $20 million per film. He also spent about $250,000 on a diamond wedding ring for Jada, as well as a brand new Ferrari as a wedding present. The event combined the wedding with a spectacular New Year's Eve party, featuring music from a cappella group Infinity. Will and Jada's wedding night was spent in a luxury hotel overlooking Baltimore's Inner Harbour, followed by a honeymoon in Miami – Will's favourite city, which would feature in a song on his next album.

Marriage was not the end of the story, however – Jada had further news for Will. 'One day we got engaged,' he remembered, 'and the next we discovered we were pregnant.'

The birth of Will's second son in June 1998 – named Jaden, after his mother – was to affect him as much as Trey's birth had. 'Having two kids, it's like I'm a real dad now,' said Will. 'I took it seriously before, but now there's a whole other dynamic that kicks in. Now, I gotta really go to work.'

Will already shared the upbringing of Trey with Sheree Zampino, proving his commitment to his extended family, but his divorce had taught him that family life had to be worked at just as hard as a movie career. 'If there's one revelation that I've had over the last five years, it's that if I focus on my relationship the way I focus on everything else, I'll be successful at it,' he claimed. 'It's so simple, but it just took me forever to figure out. I was so blind before, so blind. You can't work fourteen hours a day, come home on the weekend exhausted and think that everything's going to be wonderful. You have to talk about it and work on it, and we do that. All the time.'

Following his success with songs from the *Men in Black* soundtrack, Will Smith was ready to return to music seriously after a break of five years. His new deal with Sony/Columbia resulted in a newly-revitalised style, combining the best of his trademark positive rap and mainstream pop. Dropping the Fresh Prince title, Will adopted the nickname Big Willie instead, titling his 1997 album *Big Willie Style*.

He was playing to the fans who had grown up with him since the late eighties, as well as a whole new generation who knew him mainly from *The Fresh Prince of*

Bel-Air and the cool intergalactic adventure of *Men in Black*. Along for the ride was Will's one time partner-in-rhyme Jazzy Jeff Townes, who produced three tracks and contributed to two others, including the hit single 'Gettin' Jiggy Wit' It'. As always, Will stayed true to those who were around when his career started and had not abandoned him when his first flush of success ended in near bankruptcy.

'If there's one revelation that I've had over the last five years, it's that if I focus on my relationship the way I focus on everything else, I'll be successful at it.'

The rap world had changed by the late nineties, but the violent subculture associated with it had not gone away. The deaths of rappers Biggie Smalls and Tupac Shakur in 1997 had been the most public manifestation of this malaise. Will even found himself connected to these events in the form of bizarre rumours linking him with Biggie Smalls, AKA Notorious B.I.G., with whom he'd been spending time just hours before the rapper's death in a shooting incident.

The success of *Big Willie Style* – his best-selling album selling over three million copies – and 'Gettin' Jiggy Wit' It' reaching the number one spot on the *Billboard* charts revived some of the old criticisms of Will Smith practising a form of safe, commercial, 'white' rap, far removed from the real thing. While Will had counted Tupac Shakur among his friends – and others in the rap world, including Biggie Smalls, Puffy Combs and Babyface, as 'good acquaintances' – he was not going to change his positive, populist style just to gain street credibility. 'Rappers like to talk about keeping it real, you know?' noted Will of his critics. 'But it's like, Nigga, no you *ain't!* If you take all of the past five years of gangsta rap records, there's no way that those records are indicative of the lifestyle that those people lead every day. Every last one of them niggas has cried in the last five years about something. A'ight? And if it ain't in your record, you ain't keeping it real, you know what I'm sayin'? To me, that whole keepin' it real concept is hypocritical bullshit.'

For Will, the negative attitude of so much rap was a turn off. 'When I think of gangsta rap, people *think* they are doing what Tupac and Biggie were doing, but intellectually, spiritually, they're falling short of the mark.'

Big Willie Style showed a more mature Will Smith at work. His experiences in the ten years since starting his life in showbusiness all fed into the songs, tackling love, marriage, fatherhood, divorce, and even his own fame. He also took the opportunity to pay homage to the music he grew up with, featuring prominent samples from seventies disco performers like Sister Sledge, Chic, Earth, Wind and Fire and Kool and the Gang.

Will's good-natured musical comeback was welcomed by music critics who seemed as fed up with the negativity of gangsta rap as Will himself. One review in *Rolling Stone* complimented *Big Willie Style* for recapturing 'the lucid energy of early eighties rap hits', while *People* was convinced that, despite his high flying career, Will Smith had 'managed to stay in touch with his Philadelphia hip-hop roots'. For *USA Today*, the attraction of Will Smith and his music was simple: 'Even when he's taking licks at his hip-hop detractors for his fun-loving style, his aim is to have a good time.' As Will himself put it, 'The essence of rap was always about partying and having fun. The best rapper was the one that could rock the house. How well you shot a gun wasn't part of the criteria.'

In the wake of *Men in Black*, Will Smith could have kicked back and had a good time. Although he knew how to relax, those around him were worried about his work rate. When he signed up to play the lead role in Tony Scott's conspiracy thriller *Enemy of the State* (1998), Jada Pinkett and Will's personal manager James Lassiter, an old friend from Overbrook High School, became worried that he simply was not taking enough time to relax. 'He is the singularly most focused person I've ever met in my life,' commented Lassiter.

Jada's concern for her husband was more personal. 'Of course, I worry about him,' she admitted. 'He's non-stop, always doing something. I tell him he needs to just sit down, be quiet, have some stillness. I say it all the time: "When do you have time to replenish all that energy? Someday, you're just gonna keel over!"'

08

BIG WILLIE STYLE

With *Enemy of the State*, Will Smith would gear his talents towards a mainstream thriller – but, in case his play-it-straight gambit did not connect with his fan following, he had the insurance of *Wild, Wild West* (1999) – an over-the-top, sci-fi inspired western – with which he aimed to capture the Fourth of July weekend for the *third* time in four years.

Enemy of the State had been in development so long that the final film carried a production credit for Don Simpson – the force behind Will Smith's *Bad Boys* action movie debut – even though he had died of a drug overdose one year earlier. Simpson and his partner Jerry Bruckheimer began developing the idea for a surveillance thriller back in 1991. 'It took a long time to get a screenplay,' noted Bruckheimer, who carried on developing the film after Simpson's death. 'We started with a simple one-line idea about a man whose "electronic identity" is stolen and manipulated. We asked a young writer, David Marconi, to come in and

Will jumped at the chance of working once again with director Barry Sonnenfeld,
in a modern take on 60's TV show The Wild, Wild West.

develop it. It grew from there to encompass the scope of institutionalised information gathering.'

For Marconi, the key to this information-age suspense yarn was to find an identifiable 'bad guy' against whom the film's hero could battle. 'After a lot of investigation, I eventually was able to come up with a boogie man – the National Security Agency,' said the writer. 'Their nickname was No Such Agency. If you take an idea like that and marry it to a *Three Days of the Condor* type of story, I thought it would turn into a good movie.'

Marconi set about bringing his story of the technological threat to privacy to life by grounding his characters in reality. His hero was Robert Clayton Dean, a likeable family-man Washington DC lawyer whose wife has a strong awareness of civil rights issues. A chance encounter with an old friend sees Dean framed for murder and caught up in a web of intrigue which wrecks his life. Behind the scheme is rogue NSA operative Thomas Brian Reynolds (Jon Voight), with ex-NSA spy Brill (Gene Hackman) coming reluctantly to Dean's rescue.

With the first draft screenplay well underway, Bruckheimer contacted director Tony Scott, who had previously worked for the producer on *Crimson Tide* (1996) and *Top Gun* (1986). Although Scott claimed an interest in the subject matter, he initially turned Bruckheimer down – only the quality of the final script finally brought him aboard.

Fascinated by the centrality of extensive secret surveillance, Scott set out to make *Enemy of the State* into a moralistic action movie, a film both action-packed and capable of dealing with substantial issues. 'I was always a big fan of *Three Days of the Condor* and *The Conversation*. The real challenge was to take this genre and re-educate the public about what goes on in the world today.'

When casting began, the director only ever had one actor in mind for the role of Robert Clayton Dean. 'I had looked at Will Smith in *Six Degrees of Separation* when he was so young,' noted Scott. 'I also looked at the bits in *Bad Boys*, *Independence Day* and *Men in Black* when he had a few serious moments, and he handled them so well and his choices during those moments were so good, I knew he could handle something more serious. I watched him grow, in terms of the drama, from the first week of shooting to the last.'

As with his two previous SF-adventure movies, Will's role had not been written specifically as a black character. Once again, the producers hoped his audience appeal would transcend any issues of race. *Enemy of the State* was to be Will's first straight drama since *Six Degrees of Separation* – while it had its lighter moments, the audience had to be convinced by Will Smith playing a role in which he could not fall back on comedy antics.

'This is my leap into new territory,' said Will. 'There are no special effects, no aliens about to attack Earth. This film is serious business, and it's my first shot at playing a normal character that everyone can identify with. I can't use any comic attitude to make this character work – this time it's all about emotion and being able to draw on my talent.'

Having achieved initial film success with Simpson-Bruckheimer on *Bad Boys*, Will was reassured by the level of talent he would be working with: 'I'm finding you have to bet on the team. You bet on Jerry Bruckheimer, you bet on Tony Scott, you bet on Gene Hackman, you bet on Jon Voight. That will usually set you in a certain ballpark – you're not going to miss horribly. I mean, it's like if Gene is involved there's a certain level of quality that's going to be there.'

It was Scott who was determined to team Will Smith with Gene Hackman. 'Gene and Will are perfect for their roles, just in terms of their nature and temperament,' noted the director. 'Regardless of who they are in the movie, these guys are perfect role models for the characters in the script.'

'The great thing about Jerry and Tony is they gave us *Crimson Tide*, and that's the kind of feel this film has', opined Will himself. 'Political thriller would be the best description of the genre, but I'm running and jumping and falling and screaming. But there's also great acting moments.'

For his role as a Washington lawyer, Will drew inspiration from close to home – Jada Pinkett's uncle, himself a lawyer. Will knew that Jada's uncle approached his work seriously, but with a great sense of humour, suggesting a method of joining Will's dramatic talents with his flair for comedy 'My natural instincts are always comedic,' Will admitted. 'But necessity is the mother of invention and having taken that tool [comedy] away, I was forced to create something new and different. It's been a while since I did work that was emotionally demanding. This was a little harder, a little darker.'

It was not until ten days into shooting that Will realised the extent of the demands his character was going to make upon him. 'I was flipping through the script to get a sense of how many days I was going to be working,' recalled Will, 'and it started to dawn on me that the weight was on my shoulders more than ever before. This film wasn't a buddy film. It's the first time that I've been completely out front, where the story is about my character. It's just not physically exhausting, the emotional aspect can be equally daunting.'

Without a Martin Lawrence or Tommy Lee Jones to rely on for back up, Will carried the weight of most of the film's key dramatic scenes. 'I'm not expecting to be acting in the same league as these guys,' he said of his *Enemy of the State* co-stars Gene Hackman and Jon Voight. 'These guys are brilliant actors; they're established as the top men in their profession. I had almost nothing to lose and everything to gain appearing with them. What if I could hold my own and not embarrass myself? Hopefully everybody will start thinking, "Hey, this Smith guy wasn't so bad after all . . ."'

For Tony Scott, the emotional key to the film was Will Smith's natural persona. 'He plays an affable guy with a sense of humour. Audiences see him playing some tough, strong, emotional moments – doing things that, as an actor, he's never been asked to do before.'

'I think, in a lot of ways, I've gotten respect for being able to act by default,' admitted Will of his previous, populist work. 'I'm still kind of living off *Six Degrees of Separation*, I haven't really proved myself as an actor yet. That was the big reason to do this movie, because when you're sitting across a table and doing a scene with Gene Hackman, you know there's no bullshit. You have got to be ready, because, man, Gene brings fire. I love it because I truly believe that the way to be great is to associate with greatness. You hang out with Oscar winners, and people start to think you belong there. It was the same with Tommy Lee Jones in *Men in Black* – they're supposed to be better than me. I don't have to worry about exploding off the screen. All I have to do is not get chewed up. That's how I get the nerve to go out there.'

Although Will tackled a few stunts, the special effects in *Enemy of the State* were mainly added in post-production to capture the sinister edge of surveillance technology. 'We took a tour of the CIA which was just amazing', explained Will. 'It was definitely a higher-up tour – you can't just walk in there. They can call up satellite surveillance for the entire planet. Name any street corner, and they can call up tapes of everything that happened there.' He found that the real-life situation was even more advanced than anything *Enemy of the State* could depict. 'What's really amazing is that you have to imagine that anything you see in a movie is probably about ten to fifteen years behind what they actually have,' said Will.

The research visit to CIA headquarters in Langley, Virginia, as arranged by head of public affairs Chase Brandon, was supposed to be a secret. Upon arrival, however, Will found the corridors lined with secretaries and other office personnel clutching photographs and hoping for autographs. 'We were accompanied by fans on the entire four hour tour,' said executive producer Chad Oman, 'and by the time we left, Will's pants were torn, but he was none-the-worse for wear. Will was such a good sport.'

For the role of his strong-willed wife Carla, Will Smith recommended actress Regina King. Director Tony Scott was looking for an actress who would provide a contrast to Will's happy-go-lucky lawyer. 'I had to see the idea of who she was in their relationship', explained Scott. 'Once I determined that she wore the pants in the house, I knew Regina was it.' Other cast members included Lisa Bonet (*Angel Heart,* 1987), playing Robert Clayton Dean's old flame Rachel Banks, and, in extended cameos, Tom Sizemore (*The Relic, Saving Private Ryan*) as a mobster and Gabriel Byrne as an NSA agent impersonating renegade spy Brill.

Location shooting began in the autumn of 1997 in Baltimore, Maryland, continuing in Washington DC, then winding up back in Los Angeles by January 1998. To ensure authenticity, Scott actually shot some scenes using many of the miniature cameras used by the intelligence community themselves. Creating the National Security Agency headquarters, and reflecting its shadowy workings, had to be achieved, naturally, without co-operation from the agency itself.

Will Smith hoped that appearing alongside Gene Hackman in Enemy of the State *would ensure more 'serious' roles in the future.*

The action scenes – including the destruction of Brill's warehouse hideout, a frantic chase through a car tunnel and several rooftop scenes – were developed after the script was completed and production was already underway. In particular, the spectacular demolition of Brill's hideout was suggested by a location discovered by Scott – the original Baltimore Dr Pepper factory. The destruction of the building – covered by thirteen cameras – heightens the tension between Hackman's character and Will Smith's lawyer, as the latter realises he is caught up in a very different world to the one he knows.

While *Enemy of the State* is not as dark as Francis Ford Coppola's *The Conversation* (1973 – also starring Gene Hackman), it is a fast-paced thriller with great performances which manages to tackle some serious issues. Roger Ebert of the *Chicago Sun-Times* felt that 'Smith is credible as the good lawyer who is blindsided by the misused power of the state,' while the *San Francisco Examiner* opined that 'the pairing of Smith and Hackman is inspired. Smith is a young, nerdy-cool lawyer teamed with a grizzled, screw-you government operative.'

'Racism is an unfortunate part of American culture. It's something you don't accept but something you know is going to exist.'

As the most successful black star Hollywood had ever produced, Will Smith was described by the *Los Angeles Times* as one of 'a select number of African-Americans [who] have parlayed success in one field into power in the movie world'. Far from seeing his colour as an obstacle to overcome, he sees it as truly irrelevant to his success. 'It's not any more of a hindrance than it is doing anything else,' said Will of being black in Hollywood. 'Racism is an unfortunate part of American culture. It's something you don't accept but something you know is going to exist. I'm a firm believer that the smartest person wins. When I sit in meetings in Hollywood dealing with directors, producers, executives, they need me. Even before they knew they needed me, I knew they needed me. You will never hear me say some white man owes me something because of slavery. I'm not giving that kind of credit.'

Will sees the racial interchangeability of his movie roles – all originally written for white actors – as the foundation of his 'everyman' appeal. 'Like, five years ago when the producers were trying to cast me for *Independence Day*, they said, "Well, black actors don't translate internationally." And then it's the same thing with *Men in Black.* They said that *Independence Day* was a fluke. And to me that's ludicrous. It's just a thing that Hollywood believes and that they try to subscribe to.'

Having rapidly proved this blinkered attitude wrong, Will knows that as the leading black actor in Hollywood – whose name has become synonymous with multi-million dollar blockbusters – he is a symbol of positive aspiration to his peers. 'There is definitely a burden to carry,' he admits, 'but I think that responsibility has always made blacks that choose to carry the burden stronger. Jackie Robinson, being the first black ever to play major-league baseball, he wasn't just a ballplayer. He had to be extra special. That's something to deal with, but it's almost a good thing. It makes you work harder. I want to play positive characters. I want to play characters that represent really strong, positive black images. So that's the thing I consider when I'm taking a role after I decide if it's something that I want to do. At this point, I don't want to play a gangster, unless it's a role that has a different or more positive message.'

One of the seemingly unlikeliest of roles so far was about to come Will's way – once again written for a white actor, he would step into the shoes of the character James T. West in the blockbuster remake of 1960's TV series *The Wild, Wild West*.

When Barry Sonnenfeld signed on to direct the long-mooted film version of the hit American TV series, he only had one name in mind for the lead role of secret agent Jim West: his *MiB* star, Will Smith. For Sonnenfeld, agreeing to helm the movie was like taking a step back to his childhood. 'I grew up watching *The Wild, Wild West* and loving it,' recalled the director. 'It was like James Bond in the West with all these cool gadgets and sexy women every week. It was really fun for me to put my own spin on the feature film.'

The original series ran on CBS from 1965 to 1969 starring Robert Conrad as Jim West who, along with inventor Artemus Gordon (Ross Martin), battled evil in the Old West with the aid of steam-driven technology and gadgets clearly based on the immensely popular James Bond films. Two TV movies in 1979 and 1980 briefly revived the series, but it was not until 1992 that Warner Brothers began to seriously consider a big-budget film version.

Trapped in 'development hell' for many years after Mel Gibson turned it down in favour of *Maverick* (another movie update of a Western-themed TV show), undergoing many a rewrite, *Wild, Wild West* (for the film version, the definite article 'The' was dropped from the title) appeared to be simply the latest in a long line of un-made movies – until the dynamite duo of Barry Sonnenfeld and Will Smith became attached.

Will jumped at the chance to work with Sonnenfeld again, and was intrigued by the idea of a modern take on the old cowboy myths. 'I do think Barry understands how to take something that may be a little different and spin it in such a way that makes it unusual, special, fun and exciting,' he said of his director. Between them, they soon identified the characteristics of Jim West that could cross any racial divide. 'West is a man of action, very impulsive. He's straightforward, simple and direct. There's a certain way to do things, a code, and that's what he lives by.'

In *Wild, Wild West,* Government Agent James West (Will Smith) teams up with inventor and master of disguise Artemus Gordon (Kevin Kline) to track down evil genius Dr Arliss Loveless (Kenneth Branagh), who is plotting to assassinate the President of the United States. Helped by Gordon's flamboyant steam-driven gadgets, West discovers Loveless' ultimate weapon – a huge walking spider-tank dubbed the Tarantula. Along the way West also meets glamorously mysterious entertainer Rita Escobar (Salma Hayek), who might just be the key to defeating Loveless' diabolical scheme.

'Part of the reason I've been successful is that I know people. I can just tell if it's going to work, and I had that with Salma. You can get blinded by her beauty, but she's hilarious.'

The outrageous plot and flashy gadgetry of *Wild, Wild West* were obvious attractions for both director and star, but equally important was the human component. To Sonnenfeld, Kevin Kline was the ideal partner for Smith's hero, beating George Clooney and Johnny Depp to the role. 'I wanted an actor's actor for this role,' noted Sonnenfeld. 'West and Gordon are as opposite as they can be. Jim's theory is shoot first, ask questions after while Artemus is all about planning and never about action.'

With the heroes in place, Sonnenfeld had to find an actor capable of carrying off the comic-book villainy of evil Dr Loveless. His unusual choice was Shakespearean actor-director Kenneth Branagh: 'We needed a nineties villain who would be truly threatening to our larger-than-life heroes, and British actors can play very large. Kenneth's style of performance is very enjoyable, full of energy and glee, totally believable and scary.' Surrounded by a bevy of beautiful women, Dr Loveless is confined to a wheelchair after losing his legs in a self-inflicted accident.

The leading female role was harder to fill, although Will continually recommended gorgeous Mexican actress Salma Hayek to a reluctant Barry Sonnenfeld. 'Part of the reason I've been successful is that I know people,' claimed Will. 'I can just tell if it's going to work, and I had that with Salma. You can get blinded by her beauty, but she's hilarious.' Sonnenfeld needed much persuasion however. 'Never, never, ever did she have an audition that convinced me it would work out,' elaborated the director. 'I was really worried. Each time Salma auditioned, I was concerned whether or not she'd go where I needed her to go.' Despite all the director's worries, Will's instinct would once more prove correct. 'What's shocking is how well it worked out,' Sonnenfeld admitted. 'I thought I'd figure out how to make her funny. It turned out I didn't have to – she got it right away.'

Will Smith and Kevin Kline worked well off each other in Wild, Wild West, *forming a truly comic partnership.*

The most important thing about such a 1990's-style, big budget, big-screen comic book movie is often not the ironically-witty script (supplied by S. S. Wilson and Brent Maddock) or the mannered performances of the stars, but the startling production design. Given the chance to bring weird and wonderful Jules Verne-style technology to the Old West, production designer Bo Welch (*Batman Returns*) was in his element. 'I knew the style should be big, but also totally stylised,' noted Welch. 'It's retro-science fiction with a Western backdrop. What could be more interesting to design than a science fiction world of 1869?'

One of the main challenges was the incongruously hi-tech steam train in which the two agents travel the newly formed United States of America, known as the Wanderer. 'West and Gordon have no home in the movie,' said Welch, 'so the Wanderer becomes their home and headquarters for this mission. It's also a wonderful common thread that weaves through the movie, like you are travelling with them on this adventure.'

Bo Welch designed the Wanderer as a kind of Batcave-on-rails. 'I wanted it to feel like an exclusive men's club, with a sort of very opulent, luxurious, rich quality,' he said of the interior. The train took two months to build and incorporated a flip-

Will Smith and Kevin Kline aboard their adopted home, the Wanderer.

over pool table, a state-of-the-art weapons development lab, trap doors, gattling guns disguised as lamps and a swinging mallet which deals with unwelcome guests. 'Our heroes spend a lot of time on the Wanderer,' said Sonnenfeld. 'If *Wild, Wild West* were taking place today, it would be their Gulfstream jet.'

Not to be outdone, the villain of the piece also has his brilliantly-designed contraptions – many brought to life by leading visual effects company Industrial

Light and Magic – with which to outfox West and Gordon. 'He's into machines,' acknowledged Welch of Dr Loveless, 'steam power, heavy metal and cast iron.' The villain's base is a giant cast-iron greenhouse where he plans his wicked deeds, while he also boasts a steam-driven armoured wheelchair, a tank train dubbed Black Death and the formidable 80-foot-tall spider vehicle the Tarantula. 'Loveless is a man without legs and the thing that fascinates him most is the spider. Loveless is impressed and fascinated by its abilities, so the spider is his inspiration, his signature and a recurring motif in the film,' explained Welch.

Filming, which began in April 1998, was not without incident. In August, fire broke out at the famous Cook Ranch (though no one was hurt) set outside Santa Fe, New Mexico – previously used for westerns like *Silverado* and *Wyatt Earp* – now the set for the climactic battle between Dr Loveless' Tarantula and Jim West. At the end of that month, *Newsweek* reported that Sonnenfeld had shattered his wrist during a boxing match with Will Smith. The accident reportedly happened

'That's the great thing about being an actor – as soon as you get the wardrobe on, you really start to feel the thing.'

when the director and Will were horsing around – Sonnenfeld took a swipe at Will and hit his shoulder bone by mistake, impacting on his wrist. Will reputedly felt terrible about the accident, though it was no fault of his own. An official statement by the production company, Warner, claimed that the injury happened when 'a stage door flew open, and Sonnenfeld happened to be in the way'. (Later, during post-production in February 1999, Sonnenfeld had a brush with death when his plane crash-landed at Los Angeles Van Nuys airport. 'The weird thing is that I hate to fly, and every time I get off a plane I view it as a failed suicide attempt,' said the shaken director.)

After post-production, a series of sneak preview screenings of an early cut of *Wild, Wild West* elicited a surprising amount of negative comment cards. Complaints included the fact that little mention was made in the film of Jim West's colour – something neither Will nor Sonnenfeld had initially felt was important, though it led Sonnenfeld to issue a responsive statement: 'We will absolutely address the fact that our lead character is a black man during this period in time. It's a concept that we're embracing.' Due also to requests for more slapstick comedy to make the film much more like *Men in Black*, Sonnenfeld and Warners mounted a series of re-shoots featuring Will's character. Despite this, as a show of confidence by Warners, the film was moved forward from its original release date of 2 July (covering Will's famous 'Big Willie Weekend' of 4 July) to 30 June, capturing early holiday cinemagoers and benefiting from the eventual downturn in audiences for *Star Wars:* Episode 1, *The Phantom Menace*.

Despite his character's situation in the nineteenth century, Will was determined to drag his 1990s smarts back to the past, filtering modern hip-hop street style through traditional period costumes. 'The waistcoat was the first thing that was part of my deal,' explained Will. 'I had to wear that. We also put a couple of other things with it, like the 1869 sunglasses and a tilt to the hat. That's the great thing about being an actor – as soon as you get the wardrobe on, you really start to feel the thing.'

For Sonnenfeld, the similarities between the lead character and a movie secret agent were too strong to resist underlining them. 'There's a moment in the film with Will, so handsome in this black cowboy outfit and hat. Will has broken into Loveless's party and Bai Ling as his henchwoman says, "Hello, my name is Miss East." Will taps his hat and says, "West . . . James West." It's pure Bond, but in 1869 and I love it.'

Any Will Smith event movie is not complete without a title song sung by the star, and *Wild, Wild West* was no exception. Included on this rather epic recording, which became a hit single even before the film was released, were Stevie Wonder, R&B group Dru Hill and hip-hop artist Kool Moe Dee. For the promotional video, Will starred in a seven minute mini-epic directed by Paul Hunter that built on elements from the film while telling its own story with bursts of action between the music. 'It continues the fantasy of the movie,' explained Will, 'and adds some other elements to tell another story – one that's supported by the music talents involved.' As well as Will and Salma Hayek (who volunteered to work free on the project), the 'Wild, Wild West' video featured Will's *Fresh Prince of Bel-Air* co-star Alfonso Ribeiro in a cameo. Even on the set of the film, Will Smith had never let his co-stars forget he was also a musician. 'Every day he sings,' said Salma Hayek during production. 'He has all of us singing. Beatles' songs, eighties songs . . . I've never seen so much energy.'

As the release date for his latest Will Smith feature loomed, Barry Sonnenfeld was happy he and his team had done their best to realise the potential of the remade, revamped, re-shot *Wild, Wild West*. 'It's full of action, sweeping vistas, eye-popping special effects and inventions and larger-than-life characters,' boasted the director. 'We tried to give it the biggest, most entertaining frame we could, bring the most talented performers into that frame and then let the magic and fun happen.'

Sonnenfeld and Will were hoping that *Wild, Wild West* would spawn a franchise. 'There's probably a better chance of doing a sequel to this movie than *Men in Black*,' Sonnenfeld optimistically claimed. 'With *Men in Black* it's hard financially because Steven Spielberg has so-much percent of the back end of the movie that it's very hard for there to be money for anyone else. With *Wild, Wild West*, it would be easier to have a new caper for them to solve. It's set up as a series, so you can imagine there being another villain. With *Men in Black*, I just don't see putting a new alien in there and having them drive around.'

The possibility of a *Wild, Wild West* sequel came closer with the film's $50.1 million box office take over the five-day Independence Day holiday weekend of 1999. Although the reviews were universally negative, Will Smith had once more turned the annual holiday into Big Willie weekend. The *San Francisco Examiner* noted that 'alas, the chemistry isn't here, and it's probably more the fault of the roles than the actors, who seem game enough'. *Orlando Weekly* felt that for all the spectacle and the fun performances from the leads, the film lacked depth: '*Wild, Wild West* might once have had aspirations of becoming a grand Hollywood entertainment. Along the way, though, it turned into something far more routine, a slick and predictable piece of movie making that's ultimately routine and humdrum.' '*Wild, Wild Waste*' is more like it,' carped the *Washington Post*. ' Waste of time. Waste of money and a colossal waste of talent.' Critical opinion, however, seemed as irrelevant in the face of mass popularity as the studio's initial misgivings. 'Warner Brothers was uncomfortable with me having a beard,' laughed Will, 'and said that no movie had ever been a success when the lead had a beard. And then you think about the Lincoln story. Or Moses. But when you put the Lord into it, the Lord can make it a hit.'

Whether in a *Wild, Wild West* sequel or *Men in Black 2*, Barry Sonnenfeld was sure he'd be working with Will Smith on another movie again soon. 'I've already asked him if he'd co-direct movies with me, even if he doesn't act in them' he said. 'I truly view Will as a film-making partner.'

One project the duo had under consideration was a bold departure from the big budget summer action films that they had made together in the past. A bio pic of boxer Muhammad Ali, to be entitled either *Power and Grace* or simply *Ali*, would see Will playing the man who floated like a butterfly and stung like a bee. Will has claimed that playing Muhammad Ali would be his dream role. 'I feel like Muhammad Ali – there's the story I'm tailor-made for.' The Muhammad Ali project stalled, however, despite the fact that Ali personally approved of Will as his chosen actor to play him on film: 'I'm excited about the challenge,' said Will. 'Ali wants me to do it.' However, rival projects and threatened lawsuits from those who claimed to own the rights to Ali's life story, as well as a drifting apart of Sonnenfeld and Will after the critical backlash that *Wild, Wild West* received – all played their part in killing the Sonnenfeld-Smith project. By February 2000, the Ali bio-pic had a new director attached, Michael Mann, whose previous films include *The Insider*, *Heat* and *The Last of the Mohicans*.

While Will Smith claimed he was still interested in playing the part of Ali, it was a sport of a different nature that eventually brought him back to the big screen during the year 2000 – golf. For Will was moving away from the big-budget action vehicle and launching himself into a serious and dramatic role that was almost

'Give me about ten to fifteen years and I'm going to run for President. If I can squeeze in an NBA [National Basketball Association] championship before that, I'll do it!'

spiritual in its execution. Co-starring with another teen heartthrob actor, Matt Damon, in *The Legend of Bagger Vance*, the film is based on Steve Pressfield's mystical golf novel, about a mythic golf match that took place in 1931 in Georgia between legendary golfing stars Bobby Jones and Walter Hagan and the local war-hero Rannulph Junah (Matt Damon). It focuses in on the relationship between Junah and his caddy Bagger Vance (Will Smith), a mystically wise black man who proves to be much more than just a simple caddy as he helps Junah overcome his difficulties. Pressfield's critically acclaimed novel is itself based on the Indian epic *The Mahabharata* and, more specifically, the Bhagavad Gita and is shot in and around the dreamy and atmospheric island of Savannah off the Georgian coastline. Rising star Charlize Theron plays the organizer of the tournament, Junah's former lover, while Jack Lemmon both appears in the film and narrates it with Robert Redford as director. The film is produced by Dreamworks.

The August 4th 2000 release also took Will away from his 'natural' home of the 4th July weekend. As well as the obvious attractions of the role, the other big attraction of the film was the opportunity to work with Robert Redford – a chance which Will was not going to pass up lightly.

However, this move to explore more dramatic roles did not mean that Will was planning on leaving action films behind altogether in a bid for critical acclaim after *Wild, Wild West*. In fact, although it was not the sequel fans were waiting for, Will was back in uniform (along with Rip Torn) for *Men in Black: Alien Attack*, a short film to accompany a *Men in Black* theme park ride at Universal Studios, Florida.

Will Smith (Bagger Vance) and Matt Damon (Rannulph Junah) in The Legend of Bagger Vance.

Appearing on monitors inside ride vehicles, Will acts as a guide for visitors in their fight against the invading aliens. The interactive adventure, which debuted in April 2000, climaxes with a 30-foot bug devouring the ride cars. Agent J (that's Will, of course), comes to the rescue.

'We feel we have the biggest attraction of the year, dwarfing our other rides,' claimed Universal Studios spokesman Jim Yeager. 'So it's fitting to have a star of this magnitude be a part of it – we couldn't have done it without him.'

Whether Smith and Sonnenfeld will reunite for the anticipated sequel to *Men in Black* remains to be seen. During the summer of 2000, *Galaxy Quest* writer Robert Gordon was penning a script for the anticipated follow up, but neither Smith, Sonnenfeld, or fellow MIB agent Tommy Lee Jones had deals for a sequel, according to reports in movie trade paper *Variety*. Lee Jones hadn't even participated in the shoot for the theme park tide.

Whatever he chose to do next, Will had no shortage of choices. With sequels to *Bad Boys*, *Men in Black* and *Wild, Wild West* all being possibilities, Will was also looking forward to creating roles for himself. Through his own company called Overbrook Entertainment (named after his high school) Will set about developing several projects. He planned to produce a romantic drama called *Love for Hire* for which he had written a script with his wife Jada Pinkett. The pair also intended to star in it when Universal bought the script, but thought better of it with Will reasoning that 'you don't want to put that kind of strain on a relationship.' Other projects Will was producing through his company, without necessarily starring in, included potential remakes of the horror classics *Cat People* and *Creature From the Black Lagoon*.

Even stranger was the possibility of Will and fellow actor Nicolas Cage playing a married couple in the Universal film *I Now Pronounce You Joe and Benny* (or *I Now Pronounce You Chuck and Larry*). The macho actors were to play two heterosexual firefighters who marry for insurance benefits. Cage would play a widower worried for his children's future who saves the life of Will's character. In return, ladies man Will promises to do anything – hence the unusual marriage proposal. Director Tom Shadyac, who brought Jim Carrey to prominence in *Ace Ventura, Pet Detective*, was interested in helming the unusual project. However, whether, after *Six Degrees of Separation*, Will would be willing to play with his image in such a way remained to be seen.

Even more unlikely was Will Smith stepping into the shoes of Cary Grant. *Silence of the Lambs* director Jonathan Demme had suggested Will as the star of a remake of the Stanley Donen classic *Charade* (1963) as the director and star had been looking for a project to work on together after Demme passed the sequel to *Silence of the Lambs*, over to Ridley Scott. They had considered making a movie of science fiction novel *K-Pax*, but *Charade*, unlikely as it sounds, looked like more of a possibility.

Will wasn't ignoring his resurgent musical career either, with his album *Willennium* putting him at the centre of the Millennium moment when 1999 became 2000. The album was generally well received, but some critics felt that Will was getting somewhat above himself as many of the tracks on the album centred on himself, his career and his wilder ambitions – such as his stated wish to become President of the United States. Will intended many of the hyperbolic lyrics to be seen as jokes, but some humourless listeners took them rather more seriously.

Beyond movies and music, Will was beginning to harbour other ambitions, seriously or not. While winning an Oscar at some point in the future would be the crowning glory of his acting career, he had other objectives. 'I feel like I could be the President of the United States. I really do,' he said, believing that his popularity would allow him to pursue a political career – one in which he had serious ambitions and aims. 'The thing I've learned in Hollywood is that I don't know what my limits are. I just want to be the first black President. People laugh, but I swear I'm not just saying this to be funny. Give me about ten to fifteen years and I'm going to run for President.'

In building his career at the end of the 20th century, Will Smith had been the smartest guy operating in Hollywood. Mixing in his musical abilities with the widespread popular appeal he'd gained during his years in *The Fresh Prince of Bel-Air*, he'd risen to the top of the Hollywood pecking order. His presence in a film seemed to guarantee a blockbuster box office opening weekend, a hit single and an on-screen presence like no other. Two of Will's films – *Independence Day* and *Men in Black* have earned more than $250 million each, while *Bad Boys* and *Enemy of the State* have grossed over $175 million each. He'd been dubbed Actor of the Year in 1999 by the movie exhibitors and theatre owners who gather at the annual ShoWest convention, when *Enemy of the State* became his third $100 million plus grossing film in a row. Despite it's bad press, *Wild, Wild West* achieved a $50 million opening weekend gross in the United States, finally taking almost $114 million, with an additional $85 million taken in territories outside the US and world-wide sales of Will's tie-in single from the film increased his grand total of records sold world-wide to 15 million, a feat he'd achieved in less than ten years.

By now, Will had the lifestyle to go with his success – but this time he was not about to throw it all away on flashy extravagance. He now had a wife and two children to take care of, with another on the way. In March 2000 Will and wife Jada announced that their second child together was due in November.

Admitting openly to his financial mistakes of the past was the first step for Will in taking responsibility for his family's future. 'I don't think you can say that because someone was young that what they did wasn't dumb – it was still dumb,' admitted Will of his wild spending youth at the end of the eighties.

Now he had a grand home in suburban LA – complete with a kidney-shaped pool, a small recording studio, a koi pond and a par-three golf course, the 8,000 square foot south-western style fenced-in house being 45 minutes outside LA, near

Calabasas. Will was also in the process of having a second property built near Malibu. In the drive way of his Calabasas house sat four extravagant cars – one featured a custom stereo system, a satellite navigation system, and two phone lines with a DVD player and a Sony Playstation mounted on back seats for his two kids, Trey and Jaden, to play with on longer journeys. There was no doubting that he'd made it this time.

Will also knew he had struck it lucky in marriage the second time around. Along with his kids, his wife Jada is the most important person in his life. He also knows that this time he is going to have to work at this relationship having learned from his past mistakes. 'I focus on my relationship with Jada like a soldier,' claimed Will. 'You've got to work at it. When we're together, I'm her mate, I'm her security guard, I'm her cook. I'm everything. I get turned on by working 16 hours, then completely drained coming in the house and taking the baby for an hour from her; that makes me feel strong. You have to focus on everything in your life with that type of military intensity.' Will's view of living life as a military style campaign was undoubtedly a hang-over from his own strict upbringing by his father, once a military man himself. 'The way that Jada and I run our relationship is that we sacrifice ourselves completely for the other person,' claimed Will. 'I'll come home from work and give her a massage. She knows I've worked all day, and the next day she wants so bad to do something for me.'

For her part, Jada Pinkett was not really worried that Will could not adjust to his ever growing levels of fame and popularity. Her support was more important than ever before, especially when a US national survey of teenage girls saw Will voted the most admired star anywhere, beating Tom Cruise and Jim Carrey and putting even more pressure on her husband to be a role model. 'Look at everything that has happened to him,' she noted, 'I never see him freak out. I never see him being rude to anyone. He really has his head on straight.'

Even within the family, Will Smith had to face some tough critics, like his five-year-old son Trey, who one day announced to his father: 'I don't know why people laugh at what you say, Dad. You're not really that funny.'

In the early days of a new century, Will still had ambitions that he wanted to fulfil. He loved his popular action-guy persona, but felt that the films he was making did not stretch or challenge him and he was rarely considered for the roles that might lead to an Oscar nomination. His hopes were that *The Legend of Bagger Vance* or the Muhammad Ali bio-pic might just give him that opportunity and he yearned for something like *Six Degrees of Separation* again, a film which proved tough to make and challenged him rather than one that was a breeze and fun to do. 'It was the only film I did that I didn't have fun making,' said Will of his heart-felt performance in *Six Degrees of Separation*, the role which many critics still consider his best.

After dominating three July 4th weekends in four years, Will was aware that his kind of cheerful blockbuster movies and characters might outlive their welcome. 'I'm starting to feel those rumblings,' he said of a potential anti-Will Smith backlash, the process which sooner or later afflicts all the most popular entertainers. 'That's scary, and I'm hoping that it doesn't grow beyond this. Eddie Murphy said to me: "The more you win, the more they're going to want you to lose".' Financially, Will had nothing to worry about, earning as he was $20 million per picture, with millions more coming in from TV syndication and music releases.

Beyond all the acclaim of his movie fans, the critics (who often blew hot and cold when it came to Will Smith) and the record buyers however, it was the opinions of those he worked with that Will considered most important. It was these people who saw the real Will Smith in action during the process of making movies. According to his *Wild, Wild West* co-star Kevin Kline – 'Will is the only actor with whom I've worked who is preternaturally chipper when arriving on set at 6am.'

His two time director Barry Sonnenfeld summed up Will's across the board appeal. 'I used to say that Tom Hanks is the most normal actor I've ever worked with [Sonnenfeld was the cinematographer on Hank's movie *Big*], but Will is just so special and happy.'

Will's friend and fellow performer Keenan Ivory-Wayans recognised his special quality. 'There's only 20 people in our industry who have that quality about you that is attractive to a large audience. We all wish that we had that kind of appeal.'

Despite the relative failure of *Wild, Wild West*, Will remained as bankable as ever in the year 2000, according to one studio executive who spoke to *Entertainment Weekly*. 'The guy's multi-talented. *Wild, Wild West* didn't hurt him. He's still a great investment.'

Producer of *Enemy of the State* and *Bad Boys*, Jerry Bruckheimer saw an Oscar waiting in Will Smith's future. 'I see Will making the same kind of choices that Tom Cruise did,' he noted. 'They're both very tenacious and very smart about whom they work with. Anytime you see someone put together a career like Will has, you know it's not luck. He is going to have an Academy Award before he's done. There's no doubt about that.'

For his part, co-star Gene Hackman became a genuine admirer of Will's talents and flexibility, seeing a strong future for the actor. 'He's a bright guy,' said the veteran actor of the younger newcomer. 'He can take charge of himself, which is what it takes to have a long career in this business. I don't think he's got anything to worry about.'

According to Warren Littlefield, NBC Entertainment's president who first backed Will in *The Fresh Prince of Bel-Air*, 'Will Smith is a rocketship. He took off and just kept going.'

FILMOGRAPHY:

Films

Where The Day Takes You
(1992) USA, 105 minutes.
Directed by Marc Rocco,
Screenplay by Michael Hitchcock
and Marc Rocco.
Cast: Laura San Giacomo
(Interviewer), Dermot Mulroney
(King), Robert Knepper (Rock
Singer), Will Smith (Manny),
Ricki Lake (Brenda), Lara Flynn
Boyle (Heather), Kyle
MacLachlan (Ted).

Made in America (1993)
USA, 111 minutes.
Directed by Richard Benjamin,
Screenplay by Marcia Brandwynne
and Nadine Schiff.
Cast: Whoopi Goldberg
(Sarah Matthews), Ted Danson
(Hal Jackson), Will Smith
(Tea Cake Walters).

Six Degrees of Separation (1993)
USA, 101 minutes.
Directed by Fred Schepisi,
Screenplay by John Guare, based
upon his play.
Cast: Stockard Channing (Ouisa
Kittredge), Will Smith (Paul),
Donald Sutherland (Flan Kittredge).

Bad Boys (1995)
USA, 118 minutes.
Directed by Michael Bay,
Screenplay by George Gallo
(story) and Michael Barrie.
Cast: Martin Lawrence (Marcus
Burnett), Will Smith (Mike
Lowrey), Lisa Boyle (Girl Decoy).

Independence Day (1996)
USA, 142 minutes.
Directed by Roland Emmerich,
Screenplay by Dean Devlin and
Roland Emmerich.
Cast: Will Smith (Captain Steven
Hiller), Bill Pullman (President
Thomas J.Whitmore), Jeff
Goldblum (David Levinson).

A Thin Line Between Love and Hate (1996)
USA, 108 minutes.
Directed by Martin Lawrence,
Screenplay by Kim Bass, Kenny
Buford, Bentley Kyle Evans and
Martin Lawrence (also story).
Cast: Martin Lawrence (Darnell
Wright), Will Smith (cameo only).

Men in Black (1997)
USA, 98 minutes.
Directed by Barry Sonnenfeld,
Screenplay by Ed Solomon, based
on the comic book by Lowell
Cunningham.
Cast: Tommy Lee Jones (Kay),
Will Smith (Jay), Linda
Fiorentino (Laurel).

Enemy of the State (1998)
USA, 120 minutes.
Directed by Tony Scott,
Screenplay by David Marconi.
Cast: Will Smith (Robert Clayton
Dean), Gene Hackman
(Brill/Edward Lyle), Jon Voight
(Thomas Brian Reynolds), Lisa
Bonet (Rachel Banks), Gabriel
Byrne (Fake Brill).

Wild, Wild West (1999)
USA, 120 minutes.
Directed by Barry Sonnenfeld,
Screenplay by Jim Thomas (also
story) and John Thomas, based on
the TV series The Wild, Wild West.
Cast: Will Smith (James T. West),
Kevin Kline (Artemus Gordon),
Kenneth Branagh (Dr. Arliss
Loveless), Salma Hayek (Rita
Escobar), M. Emmet Walsh
(Coleman).

The Legend of Bagger Vance
(2000) USA.
Directed by Robert Redford,
Screenplay by Richard
LaGravenese and Jeremy Leven,
based on the novel by Steven
Pressfield.
Cast: Will Smith (Bagger Vance),
Matt Damon (Rannulph Junuh),
Charlize Theron (Adele
Invergordon).

Television

The Fresh Prince of Bel-Air
USA, 147 x 30 minute episodes,
1990-96 Directed by Ellen Flacon
(pilot), Screenplay by various
writers.
Cast: Will Smith (Will Smith),
James Avery (Philip Banks),
Janet Hubert-Whitten (Vivian
Banks, 1990-93), Daphne Reid
(Vivian Banks, 1993-96).

TV Guest Appearances:
Disneyland's 35th Anniversary
Celebration (1989)
Blossom (1991)
MTV Spring Break (1995).

DISCOGRAPHY:

Albums

As DJ Jazzy Jeff and the
Fresh Prince: Rock the House
(1987), He's The DJ, I'm the
Rapper (1988), And in This Corner
(1989), Homebase (1991), Code
Red (1993). Jazzy Jeff & Fresh
Prince Greatest Hits (1998).
As Will Smith: Big Willie Style
(1997), Willenium (1999).

Singles

As DJ Jazzy Jeff and the Fresh
Prince: 'Girl's Ain't Nothing But
Trouble' (1986), 'The Magnificent
Jazzy Jeff' (1987), 'A Touch of
Jazz' (1987), 'Parents Just Don't
Understand' (1988), 'I Think I
Can Beat Mike Tyson' (1989),
'Summertime' (1991), 'Ring My
Bell' (1993),'Boom! Shake the
Room' (1993).
As Will Smith: 'Men in Black'
(1997), 'Just Cruisin'' (1997),
'Gettin' Jiggy Wit' It' (1997),
'Miami' (1998),'Wild, Wild West'
(1999), Freakin' It (2000).